"Joshua is great with my kids, one of whom has a sensory processing disorder and anxiety. He is patient but firm and helps her focus and keep trying even when she panics that she'll never get it."

-Shannon (Google Review)

"Joshua does an excellent job of managing the kids and teaching discipline while allowing them to have fun and participate in different challenges/obstacles. I love the confidence this has instilled in my son."

-Will (Google Review)

"I took my son to a birthday party at AMP Academy and it was fantastic!! The instructor/owner was an absolute doll with the kids, very patient but also held them to standards during class."

-Pamela (Facebook Review)

"Joshua is a terrific instructor who truly cares about the well being and success of his students!"

-Wendy (Facebook Review)

"My boy, who is usually so down on himself after group activities, walked away with his head held high talking about how frustrated he frequently felt but how 'we pushed right through it mom!' Joshua will sit knee to knee with him after class to talk about any meltdown he had ... and how he can make it better the next time around."

-Harley (Facebook Review)

Empowering Children for Success:

A Guide for Coaches, Mentors, Teachers, & Parents

By
Joshua Amarelo

Presented by:
AMP Academy LLC
Fall River, MA
www.ampacademygym.com

Empowering Children for Success:
A Guide for Coaches, Mentors, Teachers, & Parents

Cover Design:
Tiffany Yee - www.tiffanyjyee.com

AMP Academy LLC Logo Design:
Andrew Nasser - www.nasserdesign.com

www.ampacademygym.com
www.JoshuaAmarelo.com

ACKNOWLEDGEMENTS

For mom and dad who raised me. You taught me so many lessons, both intentionally and unintentionally. For that, I'm forever grateful. I love you both and appreciate you more than anything in this world.

For Gualter Amarelo, my brother, who always believed in me. You've always seen in me the potential I never saw in myself. You taught me to dream, create a vision, and make it a reality. Thank you for your faith in my vision for AMP Academy.

For Kaylin who has always supported my dreams. You understood when I worked a hundred hours a week to build AMP Academy and when I put every waking moment into writing this book. You've supported me in every major event in my life. Your smile brings me life and your laughter drives me every day. I know I'm a challenge. Thank you for your strength and for facing me head on.

For Mestre Tigri whose work in his local community inspired me to seek this path. The community you've built, that I'm fortunate enough to be a part of, is a gift in all of our lives. Thank you for being a friend and willing instructor, teaching me patience, understanding, humility.

Finally, and most importantly, for every single one of my students and their families that have helped me become the instructor that I am today. You are the reason I study and work so hard to perfect my craft. Your future success is the reason I built AMP Academy. I never imagined that I could be so lucky to have such an awesome group of people to call my family. Thank you for your continued trust and support in our mission.

TABLE OF CONTENTS

INTRODUCTION

This book is written for coaches, teachers, mothers, fathers, babysitters, aunts, uncles, cousins, brothers, sisters, social workers, nurses, doctors, dentists, firemen, policemen, and a thousand other professions that interact with children. Throughout this book I'll use the word "instructor" as an all-encompassing term for all of you interested in helping children develop into successful adults, for the simple reason that an instructor is quite plainly defined as "a person who teaches something." Regardless of your profession, children will look up to you and you'll have the responsibility of teaching them how to become the best version of themselves that they can be, and so you are an instructor. That means that every child with whom you interact - whether an athlete, a son or daughter, a niece or nephew, a customer at a store - is a "person engaged in learning," and so we'll refer to them as students.

By reading this book you're committing to bettering the lives of every child with whom you interact, and you're committing to working toward a brighter future for those children. My goal has always been to make the world a better place and I'm writing this book with that in mind. Some people invent new technologies that will make our daily tasks easier. Others have become police officers to combat drugs and violence and help make our society safer. Still others have become politicians focused on creating peace between nations, or activists fighting for equality, or missionaries bringing aid to those in third-world countries who need it. As I've grown older I've come to appreciate just how much we impact future generations with each interaction; thus, my contribution to making the world a better place is working with children, and helping others to work with children both effectively and affectionately so they'll achieve success throughout their lives.

Allow me to introduce myself. My name is Joshua Amarelo, public speaker, author, athlete, musician, and owner, founder, and head instructor at AMP Academy LLC, New England's largest Ninja Warrior, Parkour, and Martial Arts school, located in my hometown of Fall River, MA. As such, most of my examples will be in the context of an instructor teaching children various different skills, but it's important to recognize that every technique I offer in this book can be used regardless of your profession. Look for the relationships between my examples and situations from your daily lives where you can use the same technique for the same effect.

Before getting into the meat of the book, I should share with you a few key experiences in my life that guided me toward wanting to help every child be successful. When I tried to identify the catalyst that turned me from design engineer to working with kids I realized it was a culmination of experiences that gave me the ability and the desire to help kids the way that I do and the way you'll be able to also.

My mother was a high school drop-out and my workaholic father became an industrial painter after an abandoned attempt at starting his own auto body business, so when they decided to homeschool me and my brother after 1st Grade, it turned some heads. I schooled through the summers to catch up to my older brother, so my mom only had to manage one curriculum instead of two. Mom gave us the books to read and tests to take as part of our curriculum, and we were tasked with teaching ourselves. Having to teach ourselves taught my brother and I to go out and search for the information we wanted, and it gave us the opportunity to be creative and figure things out on our own.

We'd always come up with crazy ideas and we'd work through them together. Sometimes they worked out, like when he suggested that we could double the size of a K'NEX model by just replacing every piece with the next size up. From that idea, we built a four-foot tall fully functional crane that rotated, raised and lowered, opened and closed, and had an elevator operated by an RC motor for our action figures. Sometimes they didn't work, like when I suggested making paint by

3

putting crayons in the microwave on a paper plate. Mom didn't think it was funny, but I learned a valuable lesson from that experience: Melting crayons doesn't make paint - it makes a mess.

Even in writing this book, I'm learning. As I look fondly back on old memories with new eyes, I finally understand what I never did then - that experiential learning is the most effective learning. Being homeschooled, teaching myself, and making my own mistakes had life-altering effects on how I grew up and how I've developed my methods for working with kids, which we'll be jumping into shortly.

Ripley's Believe It or Not opened the world of Parkour to me in the 2001 episode featuring a French group known as "Yamakasi." There were no schools for Parkour at that time, so I just did what I've always done and taught myself. My technique crystalized as YouTube started to grow and more and more videos were posted that I could study. I had no idea when I started teaching myself parkour that over a decade later it would be the avenue I used to teach children healthy habits for a successful future. Think about your past experiences. What unassuming experience can you use to have the greatest impact on children's success?

While attending the University of Massachusetts Dartmouth in October of 2011, I was fascinated when I saw a demonstration of Capoeira - an Afro-Brazilian martial art that incorporates music, dancing, and acrobatics with self-defense. I joined the UMASS Dartmouth Capoeira Club, and Capoeira quickly took over my heart. I came to love it for its physical challenges as much as for the incredible community of caring and welcoming people that I found in it. When I graduated in 2013 with my degree in Rhetoric and Communications, I continued my capoeira training with Grupo Ondas at New Wave Martial Arts & Fitness in Warwick, RI under Mestre Tigri, the first ever Cape Verdean capoeira mestre by night, and a doctor of psychology with a focus in children's education by day.

I began unofficially studying under Mestre Tigri when I started helping with his kids capoeira classes. Even before this, I observed and studied his teaching techniques, comparing them with other instructors I'd had, be it in capoeira, managers, college professors, etc. I learned dozens of techniques from him and my fascination with teaching soon led me to researching psychology, neuro linguistics, and non-verbal communication. I studied how these affected our everyday interactions with others and started experimenting with ways I could incorporate them into teaching kids classes to help children develop success-oriented mindsets.

I still remember the conversation with my instructor that changed my entire life. It was in the wee hours of the morning in the warmth of summer during our annual capoeira graduation celebration. After hearing the incredible work that Mestre Tigri did for his community - not just his community of students, not even the entire community of capoeira, but what he contributed to his local communities of Providence and Warwick - I came to love and appreciate him for how much emphasis he put on bettering his communities. Mestre Tigri was my inspiration for what I wanted to become for my own community in Fall River.

I made a pact to never give up on Fall River despite its reputation. You see, I know the history of my city and how it was a hub in the 1920's, prized for its textile industry. While textiles are a thing of the past for our city, this city can be awesome again, and it all starts with helping the youth to see their own potential, to see their strengths and the opportunities that most people never see and therefore never take advantage of. This is my message for all children, and all adults, everywhere: If you open yourself to opportunities, opportunities will open themselves to you.

In 2015, I opened AMP Academy LLC in Fall River, MA, where we currently offer classes for Ninja Warrior, Capoeira, Stunt & Fight Choreography, Parkour & Freerunning, and Tumbling & Tricking. My students call me Polvo, which means Octopus, the nickname I earned from my years of training capoeira. In the nearly five years since opening AMP Academy, I've personally worked with nearly 10,000 kids, including my keynote speeches I've presented at local elementary and middle schools on having a Parkour Mindset, which is a success mindset presentation geared toward children and helping them overcome fears and obstacles.

Finally, that brings us to today, in 2020, where I've decided to share with you a few techniques I've developed after nearly a decade of studying human interaction and child development. Most of these techniques are based on my personal experience and study and may not reflect the opinions of those I've studied under or other professionals. Despite my years of experience teaching, I am still a student of the craft and ever will be a student of the craft, always growing and finding better ways to teach my students. We use these techniques every day at AMP Academy and I can tell you for certain that they have always worked. I consistently get parent feedback that our classes have helped their children perform better in school, have greater focus at home, be more respectful to others, get along better with siblings, and build their confidence in their bodies and their minds. I'd like for you to be able to offer those same successes to your own students.

As a former design engineer, I know what it takes to build something. Proper study, understanding, experimentation, and finally putting the highest quality of everything into the final project is the best way to create something strong that will last through the ages. Obviously, children are not machines to be assembled, however there are certain things we can do as instructors that will strengthen or weaken our students based on our decisions and actions. Our goal, then, is to engineer the best version of people that we can, physically, ethically, morally, psychologically, emotionally, and intellectually.

This book will discuss a number of things to consider as you work with children, and will also help with parenting, since coaching and teaching allow us to take the role of a parental figure for a significant portion of a child's life. Oftentimes, instructors can have a more resounding impact in a child's development simply because we aren't actually their parents.

Most parents probably notice that their children listen to pretty much anybody else before listening to them for life advice. The reason for this could be argued in an entire book in itself, but I believe it's predominantly because children see their parents in all their glory and all their shame. In a child's mind, especially in the mind of an adolescent who has begun to formulate their own thoughts and opinions of the world around them, why should they listen to somebody whose every mistake they've witnessed and felt the effects of those "failures?" I vividly remember having that very conversation with my brother when I was just fifteen years old.

We instructors, as humans, are just as "flawed" as a child's parents, but our students don't see our every mistake or the effects of our failures. They see only the good, that we have more skill than them, that we have more knowledge than them, that we are closer to the person they want to be than they themselves are. And that puts us in a position of influence over them. It's a huge responsibility and one that you're clearly taking seriously if you've sought out the information in this book.

So, thank you again for the positive impact that you're making on children's lives. Thank you for being a part of this mission to make the world a better place for the next generation. Thank you for being a person who cares enough to always seek growth and find ways to better your craft so you can have the greatest impact possible on the future. You will be the reason so many children will grow into caring, intellectual, healthy, and successful adults.

ROLE MODELING, ETHICS, & MORALS

Before diving into the techniques I'll share in this book, we must first discuss the ethical and moral responsibility that comes with having this knowledge. The things I share in this book are intended to help children become successful adults. I'll repeatedly express how much power we have when it comes to the futures of the youth we encounter, and I take these responsibilities very seriously. The actions we take when working with children will positively or negatively impact their entire lives, not just their childhoods. How we interact with our students will affect their entire mindsets from youth into adulthood.

Our fears, angers, frustrations, and how we handle every situation will forever change the way that these children experience life. A positive or negative word will change their perceptions of the world and what they can or should expect from themselves. Everything we do as instructors will impact the students we interact with on a daily basis. I'm writing this book because it's not only my interactions with my students that will impact their lives, it's also yours and the actions of every other person they encounter.

We have a responsibility to give our students the best chance possible to succeed. Take the knowledge in this book and use it for good. As Spiderman's Uncle Ben always said, "With great power comes great responsibility," and this book will give you the power to build people up or to destroy them. Use this information only for the betterment of everybody you come into contact with. Leave every person better than when you found them.

Children put the people they look up to on pedestals and will always try to mimic them. We don't need to look any further than when a child sees his father shaving and wants to put the shaving cream on his face too, or when a child sees their mother putting on lipstick and one day the mother finds that child with lipstick all over their face. I remember being younger and wanting a briefcase because my dad used one for church, and I wanted to be just like him. My grandfather wore a very specific kind of hat and I begged my mom for one when I was only six years old - I bought one for myself after he passed away because that love and admiration never leaves us. For as long as I can remember, my favorite number has always been the number "8" simply for the reason that it was the quarterback's number on my uncle's favorite football team. I didn't even watch football, much less have a favorite team! But I did have a favorite uncle, and he was a great role model to me.

Regardless of our careers, we're role models for children and they will always try to mimic us. The things they see us do will influence their entire futures. In fact, a highly influential study performed by psychologist Albert Bandura during his 1961 through 1963 focus on children's behavior exemplifies this. This experiment and its variations became known as the Bobo Doll Experiment. A Bobo Doll is an inflatable toy weighted with sand at the bottom, so it stands itself back up when tipped over.

During this experiment involving 36 boys and 36 girls between the ages of 37 months and 69 months old, an evenly male and female group of 24 were exposed to aggressive interactions with the Bobo Doll, 24 were exposed to non-aggressive interactions, and 24 were a control group exposed to no interactions. As predicted, children exposed to the video of aggressive interactions were more likely to be aggressive toward the Bobo Doll than those exposed to non-aggressive interactions.

Another fascinating aspect of the study is that children are more likely to mimic a member of the same sex than they are to mimic a member of the opposite sex. Like follows like. The boys averaged 104 aggressive interactions after exposure to an aggressive male role model, while only averaging 48.4 aggressive interactions when exposed to an aggressive female role model. Girls showed a similar change based on the role model's sex, though the disparity was not as extreme, averaging 57.7 average aggressive interactions after witnessing an aggressive female role model compared to only 36.3 after witnessing a member of the opposite sex.

The most important lesson this experiment teaches us as instructors is that children mimic behavior they witness, particularly when the behavior is performed by somebody similar to themselves (i.e. same sex, same clothing, same music preference, same taste in food, etc.). Knowing this, it's vital that we always be the best version of ourselves in front of them.

This isn't to say that we should ever lie to a child about who we are. We are human and we get sad, become upset, experience difficult situations, and make mistakes all the time. When we falsify who we are and pretend that we're perfect, a student will latch onto the first failure they see and it will destroy their opinion of us, making them lose any respect we've gained. I tell my students every day that I'm not perfect.

Even in designing AMP Academy's own parkour curriculum and ranking system, I didn't give myself the highest rank. I'm more skilled than most of my students, yes, but there are thousands of people in this world that are better than me at parkour. I'm just a man on my own journey of learning, who happens to have more information and experience than my students, so I'm sharing it. I'm not perfect and my student's shouldn't assume that I am. It's the same thing with this book.

My techniques work, and I'll continue to refine them over the years, sharing the lessons I learn with those who want to become better instructors without making the same mistakes I have.

When I say to present the best version of ourselves, I mean that we have multiple versions of ourselves. Around the children whose lives and futures we are responsible for, we should always present to them the best possible version of ourselves, the ideal version of ourselves, the version of ourselves that we most want to be in life, the version of ourselves that will help develop children into the best versions of themselves also. Be positive, be optimistic, be encouraging, be nice to everybody, be polite. None of these things are lies. These are just goals that our students can see and work toward themselves, incorporating those success-oriented habits into their own lives.

It's our responsibility to be conscious of how we interact with children, particularly given the power dynamic of us being their instructors. Let's briefly look at the 1971 Stanford Prison Experiment, which sought to glean a better understanding of power dynamics and authority. In this study, psychologist Philip Zimbardo flipped a coin to assign Stanford University students the position of prison guard or prison inmate. It was essentially designed as a roleplaying experiment to see how power affected those who held it, however the experiment was shut down after only six days due to reports of the "guards" psychologically abusing and torturing the "prisoners."

This study indicates that some people, when put in a position of power, may abuse that power. The first example that comes to my mind is cheerleading coach Ozell Williams in 2017, who was fired after video footage leaked of him forcing his students into painful splits that their bodies weren't ready to handle, instructing the victims' teammates to hold the victims' hands and thus be complicit in this abuse against minors. What this coach did is indefensible and unforgivable. It physically disgusted me seeing that footage on the news, and quite frankly, more than mere firing was warranted in that situation. It still sickens me to this day how somebody could misuse their position to harm the children they're supposed to protect.

We are responsible for our students. We must, for the good of every student, keep their physical, emotional, and psychological wellbeing in mind. Yelling at a child is never necessary or permissible from an instructor to another person's child. A simple conversation helping the child to understand why you're upset is perfectly acceptable and has far better results. If you're in a position of authority, remember that children appreciate your respect, and if you consistently show a child respect, they'll consistently return it, and you'll see better behavior because of it.

The Milgram Experiment is another compelling experiment dealing with power widely accepted in the scientific community. This Yale University study done in 1963 by Stanley Milgram sought to determine whether "obedience" was a legitimate justification for generals during the World War II genocide committed by the Nazis. In this experiment, Milgram wanted to find out how atrociously a person would act when directed to do so by somebody in a position of power.

The experiment consisted of all male participants ranging between the ages of 20 and 50 drawing lots to determine which would be the "learner" and which would be the "teacher." It was rigged so that participants were always selected as the "teacher" and an actor was used to play the "learner" in each scenario. The "learner," an accomplice referred to in the experiments as "Mr. Wallace," was taken into a separate room and hooked up to electrodes. In the experiment, if the "learner" made a mistake, the "teacher" would administer a shock to him. Each incorrect response would lead to a higher voltage shock, ranging from 15 volts, labeled "slight shock," up to 450 volts, labeled "danger - severe shock."

If a "teacher" refused to administer the shock, the experimenter located in the room with the "teacher" would use four levels of prodding to direct the "teacher" to continue:

- Prod 1 - "Please continue."
- Prod 2 - "The experiment requires you to continue."
- Prod 3 - "It is absolutely essential that you continue."
- Prod 4 - "You have no other choice but to continue."

By the end of the experiment, 65% of participants shocked the "learner" at the maximum 450 volts, while 100% of participants administered the shock up to 300 volts. Milgram replicated this experiment under 18 different scenarios to see whether a different situation would change the outcome only to find that the results were overwhelmingly consistent. What this indicates is that most people will do what an authority figure tells them to do even if they don't agree or do not want to do so.

Keeping ethics in mind, how does this affect our education of children? It's further proof that not only will adults do what they're told when directed by an authority figure, particularly a uniformed authority figure, but we can then infer that children are the same way with adults since everybody older than them is an authority figure. We have to take responsibility for the way children perform. Students trust us as instructors, and it's our ethical and moral responsibility to ensure the successful future of a child by teaching them the right way. We can't take advantage of our power and the trust that children put in us. We must ensure that every interaction keeps our students' future success in mind.

When we say things out loud, they have more sticking power. What's in your head, you can pretend was never said. You can forget about it easily, do nothing, and not feel any sense of obligation, failure, or guilt for having given up. But for whatever reason, when we say things out loud, it becomes real, and it becomes even more real when we write it down. Because of that sticking power, it's uncomfortable to do what I'm about to ask of you, but if you do, that sticking power follows you always.

If you're ready to commit to being an awesome instructor, whether coach, teacher, or parent, and you want to live every day so that you're giving the most you can to every child in every interaction, then say these words out loud: "I recognize the power my thoughts and actions have on every child's future. I promise to do my best to be the best version of myself in every interaction with every child to ensure that they have the best opportunity to become the best version of themselves."

Key Takeaways

- Children are people. If you respect them, they'll respect you.
- Be the best version of yourself so students can become the best versions of themselves.
- Take responsibility for the way your students perform.

NEURO LINGUISTIC PROGRAMMING

Have you heard of the Butterfly Effect? No, not the movie with Ashton Kutcher, but the actual theory of the Butterfly Effect. The theory essentially states that a small, seemingly inconsequential and unrelated act can have greater impacts on a complex structure. It's illustrated by the imagined concept of a butterfly flapping its wings and causing a windstorm. Neuro Linguistic Programming is like those imaginary wings.

Neurolinguistics and Neuro Linguistic Programming (NLP) is something I'll bring up a lot in this book, though it's not in most people's vocabulary. At their core, neurolinguistics and Neuro Linguistic Programming refer to the power of words. Some of you may have heard things like, "the power of positive thinking," or, "words have power." These are both along the lines of what Neuro Linguistic Programming

(NLP) actually is.

We all recognize the difference between the whole "glass half full" versus "glass half empty" example, which indicates that two people could look at the same partially-filled glass of water and have two completely different opinions of it, though both are right. One person would insist that the glass is half full, thus seeing a more positive potential, that the glass could be empty but it is instead partially filled. Conversely, the other would insist that the glass is half empty, thus seeing a more negative potential, that the glass could be full but is instead partially empty. The latter sees the draining of the glass, the steady decline, while the former sees the glass being filled and it's steady growth to its fullest potential.

The concept behind neurolinguistics is not that our words have the power to change a situation - it's that our words, like the flutter of a butterfly's wings, have the power to change our perception of a situation, thus allowing us to react in a different way that can allow us to make the most it. NLP takes the concepts of neurolinguistics and teaches us to program our own minds (or the minds of others) to perceive the world a certain way unconsciously. The "programming" part of it refers to its automation inside our own minds. It's the idea of being mindful with the words you use every day until your unconscious mind starts doing that work for you on its own.

In general, there is our conscious mind, the mind that we actively use to think throughout our days and make decisions, and then there is our unconscious mind, which harbors secret unintentional prejudices and deep-seated beliefs. Sigmund Freud spent most of his professional career studying the unconscious mind and determining how the experiences stored there from childhood affect us in our everyday lives.

Things in our unconscious minds are typically things we witnessed in our youths about how the world is supposed to be. For instance, in our unconscious mind, we have a definition of success that we've never consciously thought about. We know what success looks like in our minds, but we can't quite put it into words to explain to others. Our idea of success is based on things that we see on TV or in movies or things that were fed to us by our parents and grandparents when we were young. You can pull that information forward into your conscious mind, but it takes a bit more effort than the active thoughts in your conscious mind.

Knowing that childhood experiences burrow their ways into our unconscious minds perfectly exemplifies the urgency for healthy neurolinguistics during the five stages of a child's development. During the first two stages of a child's development, they learn mostly through osmosis. They mimic their parents without real in-depth thought as to why they do what they do or think what they think. This is where most of our unconscious beliefs are developed, but there is still opportunity to help develop a child's unconscious programming for success.

Age	Stage	Development
0 months - 3 months	Newborn	Response to external stimuli, such as grabbing your finger when you place it by their hand.
3 months - 1 year	Infant	Basic motor skills, such as head and hand movements, sitting, crawling, and picking things up.
1 year - 3 years	Toddler	Intermediate motor skills, such as walking, jumping, climbing stairs, and drawing.
3 years - 5 years	Preschool	Refine motor skills, such as dressing themselves, drawing in more detail, running, and climbing.
5 years - 12 years	School Age	Interpersonal skills, such as friendships, responsibilities, confidence, and independence.

Toward the end of the second stage, moving into the third stage, children learn more by exploration. This is where it's dangerous for a child to have "helicopter parents" - the kind of parents who want to protect their child from everything and never give them the opportunity to learn from their own mistakes. I expressed in the introduction how important it was for my development as a child to be able to make my own mistakes, like with the crayons in the microwave. Making mistakes is what teaches us to make better decisions. Protecting a child from making mistakes is equal to preventing them from learning valuable lessons.

What this means in terms of NLP is that younger children are more open to positive influences that will affect their entire futures. They are also more open to negative influences, so it's important to always keep your word choice on track when interacting with them. Remember that children will mimic you. If you use negative words and phrasing, that will become their programming and that's how they'll run through life. If you use positive words and phrasing, you'll program them for success. You'll want to work on your own internal programming so you can help your students to run a positive program in their lives also.

In the study of NLP, particularly in the success world, there are a few words that are considered taboo because they're said to communicate helplessness to the unconscious mind. Words like "can't," a word teeming with helplessness, should be replaced with "won't" or "refuse to," words that give power back to a child - it's not inability that prevents them from accomplishing something - it's choice. The words "I need to do this" should be replaced with "I want to do this," or "I'm going to do this. "Needs are imposed upon you, but desire and decisiveness are empowering. A "problem" is something that nobody wants to deal with - it's something that happens to somebody - but a "challenge" is fun to overcome, and something we set for ourselves. These minor tweaks to our language as we speak to children can make a huge difference in how they perceive the world.

I once heard somebody say, "The problem precedes the perceived problem," meaning simply that what you think went wrong is only a symptom of what actually went wrong. "My car ran out of gas" may seem like the problem, but the real problem was that "I didn't fill the car with gas, so it ran out." The car running out of gas didn't happen to me - I caused it. If we want children to succeed in their futures, we have to look at how we're interacting with them now. Are we taking responsibility for our actions? Are we teaching them to do the same? Are we giving them excuses or are we empowering them? We are either going to be an obstacle to our students' success, or we're going to be a foundation for their success.

My goal with this book is to ensure that we are only ever the foundation of a child's success, so take your words seriously. Think them through. Understand that the way you say things matters and could mean an entirely different life for yourself and your students. A single word is the flutter of a butterfly's wings.

Key Takeaways

- Practice a positive mindset in your own life if you want to develop a positive mindset in others.
- Choose empowering words, like "want" and "will" instead of "need" or "should."
- Start looking at causes rather than effects. What led to the result?

BUILDING RAPPORT

I'll talk a lot about how to keep classes structured and organized, and you may wonder how that contributes to a child's future success. Trust me, it does. Remember that every single interaction affects students' futures. The advice I give for keeping a class organized ultimately builds habits that will lead to success, like discipline, self-control, interpersonal skills, and trust. Even if you don't lead a group class or aren't a teacher, this is still great knowledge for you to have. As a parent, your kids might have groups of friends over. As aunts and uncles, you might babysit or entertain kids at family gatherings.

As I said in the introduction, I run a physical education program for students outside of regular schooling, so all of my advice and techniques are given through that lens. Each of these techniques can be fashioned for any situation - you just have to look for the moments that you can fit them in. Regardless of your field, building rapport is by far the most important first step of working with kids. In its most basic sense, building rapport is developing a positive relationship with somebody.

25

It's helping somebody get to know what kind of person you are so they can decide whether to like or trust you. When a child first meets you, they know nothing about you. They don't know if you're a serious person or if you like to laugh and make jokes. They don't know if you're going to be mean, if you're going to hurt them, or if you're going to be their friend and play with them. They don't know if they should be afraid or if they should be a friend.

You'll handle rapport-building differently based on how old each student is, but ultimately, whether parent, child, or adult student, each person wants to know you're a good instructor. Everything you do in every interaction will build rapport or harm rapport. Students will continue to get to know you beyond the first interaction, obviously, but first impressions are the most important since it will prime them to be open to your feedback, education, and knowledge in the future.

High-Fives

High-fives are my favorite technique for building rapport with students. Fist-bumps are another option, but they're more reserved and don't bring the same kind of automatic positive energy. They can be effective for maintaining rapport after a relationship has been established, but high-fives all the way for starting a relationship. The way I do this, of course, varies based on a person's age and their level of comfort in the new situation and setting. High-fives make people feel welcome in their new environment and work great for pulling people out of their shells, no matter how old, shy, or nervous they are when they first walk into a new place.

Why are high-fives such an effective technique for building rapport?

There are a few reasons for this, the first of which is science! High-fives are scientifically proven to increase dopamine levels in our brains. Dopamine is a neurotransmitter that your nervous system uses to communicate with your brain. It's the "feel-good" chemical associated with pleasure that makes us happy and fends of depression. If you're ever in a low energy mood or don't feel like doing anything, giving a series of high-fives is a great way to boost dopamine, which should help you get past that barrier and into a better mood.

Don't believe me? Think about it. When do you see high-fives? When a teammate gets a point. When a coworker tells you about their latest promotion. When your friend gets a good grade on an important test. When somebody lands a new trick for the first time after hours of drilling it. When you're at a restaurant watching a playoff game and your team gets a touchdown or scores a basket. When it's a game night with friends and your team guesses correctly during Pictionary despite how bad at drawing you might be.

A high-five is something that you see all the time when something positive happens. Sometimes you'll see random outbursts of strangers hugging strangers at football games when their team wins or gymnastics meets and tricking gatherings when an unbelievable acrobatic combo has been landed, but that's obviously not acceptable in most situations, and it absolutely wouldn't be when first meeting a new student, particularly a child. So a high-five it is!

Giving a high-five immediately associates the interaction as a positive experience before the student has even tried out whatever you're teaching. The contact establishes a physical connection, which builds trust and allows the high-five to work as a "foot-in-the-door" method for things like spotting or helping with assignments in the future - more on that in the chapter on spotting and supporting later.

This works great with students eight and under, but it also works just as effectively on older students, particularly if that student is shy. I can't count the amount of times I've had students come in for their first class only to have the child hiding behind their mother's leg, peeking around so they could see what was happening.

Ages 8 and Under

The first thing to do is have high energy in your voice, particularly with younger kids, and be super expressive with your face. Invite them in with a wave of the arm and gesture with your head. Most of the time this won't work if a child is hiding behind a parent, but it sometimes does. If they're still too nervous to jump in, make a really expressive face as if you're shocked or maybe even offended that they don't want to come in, then go right back to smiling.

At this point, make a concession and say, "All right. Can I at least have a high-five?"

Bring your hand close enough to them that they can stay behind their parent's leg. They'll be more comfortable if they don't have to do anything but lift their arm. Usually, you'll have a lazy high-five where they're really not interested in it. That's okay. This still works.

Next, give a quick word of encouragement and suggest the next step. "Nice! Now how about a double high-five?"

The word of encouragement will put a smile on their face because they'll feel good about giving a good high-five, even if they did a lazy one. They'll end up giving an even better one next time just to prove that the first one was nothing. The new student will have to come out from behind their parent in order to use both hands for the double high-five. This breaks the barrier they'd been using their parents as and it shows them that they're still safe. At this point, dopamine is doing its job and the student is starting to have some fun.

Give another word of encouragement - I like to amplify it with some surprise. "Whoa! That was even better. All right, how about this?"

Next, you'll want to set up a challenge. They're excited because they impressed you already and they want to keep impressing you. So, put your hands back to back and hold them out. The child will look at it in confusion for a second, trying to puzzle out what you want them to do, but then they'll see that you're trying to get them to give you a high-five in a weird way.

Be impressed, then offer another challenge, like your hands stacked on top of each other. Repeat with another challenge, like one hand high and one hand low, patty-cake style. At this point, the child will be laughing and smiling and ready to join in.

Just say, "Oh, yeah, I can already tell you're gonna be awesome at this. Come on, let's get in there so we're not late!" The child will be much more ready to get started. They'll be more comfortable in the new setting and will know you're a friend. They'll have started the day with a bunch of successes by impressing you with their totally awesome high-fiving skills and they'll be ready to challenge themselves more.

Ages 13 and Over

Wait, what happened to Ages 9-12? Don't worry, we'll get to that. It's easier for all of us this way - trust me.

Most of the time, you don't have to worry about convincing an adolescent or adult to join class because they usually aren't there unless they want to be. Still, building rapport is important for them to be open to your feedback. The basic high-five thing works just as well for them and my best recommendation is to treat them like you've already been friends for years.

Ask them about why they're taking your class, if they have any experience, what their favorite anime is, who their favorite character was on a TV show, or anything else they might relate to. Finding something in common will help them be more comfortable since they're around like people and they'll see that they already have a friend in this new environment. Offer a quick compliment on their band shirt, funky hair, cool glasses, or unique necklace.

"Oh, I love that band!"

"Your hair is awesome!"

"Those glasses are epic - you look like a Kingsmen or something!"

"I really like that necklace - I wish I could pull off jewelry like you."

During warm-ups or stretches, point out something good about them, whether it be their form, technique, work ethic, or even just the smile on their face as they're doing it. All these things will make new students feel more welcome. It demonstrates that you're paying attention to them, that you're interested in who they are, and that you want to get to know them. When you invest time in somebody else, they'll want to invest time in you.

Ages 9 through 12

Yeah, I know it's weird to put these out of order, but it's easier to understand the two extremes and then recognize that for this age group you'll want to treat each student on a more individual basis somewhere in the middle of the other two age groups, depending on how they present themselves during your first interaction.

Ages 9-12 are going to be at different places in their maturity process and there's a happy medium between the two extremes, one very hands-on and the other more hands-off. For this age group, you really have to play it by ear. For some, the high-five challenges will be better. For others, the conversation will be. You'll want to read the person to decide which is best.

In either case, always start with the high-five. The high-five is going to get things rolling smoothly and it's going to be a quick way to get students to like you. When students like you, they're more likely to listen to you in classes, so this is a very important step.

Handshakes

Handshakes are a more professional version of a high-five. These work extremely well with parents and with people in their twenties and up, although if it's a prospective student entering a class for the first time I still prefer a good high-five to get the energy up. Handshakes are a great way to establish trust and demonstrate respect, which helps parents be more comfortable having their children work with you.

I've also had some students who just aren't interested in high-fives, though these are pretty rare. For these students, a good old-fashioned handshake is great for them too. The types of kids that prefer a handshake to a high-five are typically the kind who like numbers and details. They're the kinds of students who will listen to every word you say in class to make sure that they don't miss out on anything.

When shaking someone's hand, there are a few important things to keep in mind.

First: Smile and Maintain Eye Contact

Don't look away when you shake a person's hand. It communicates discomfort, low confidence, and untrustworthiness, all bad things when meeting a student or their parents. If you're not confident in your position, how can I trust you to teach my child? A good instructor should be comfortable in their environment and have confidence in the subject they're teaching. Only then can a parent trust you with their child.

Second: Vertical Hand, Palm to the Side

Placing your hand on top with your palm down is a very dominant posturing and can bother a lot of people, making them feel like they're being manhandled. It's not a great way to build a relationship. Placing your palm on the bottom with the palm up is a very submissive posturing and can sometimes lead to people thinking you're less confident. However, this is also a sign of service, so it can be perceived in a good way too. I much prefer the neutral posturing of having the hand vertical with my palm faced out to the side. This communicates that you see the person as an equal. You're not better than them and they're not better than you. It's the best way to establish an equal footing and build rapport.

On occasion, I've dealt with people who come in and go for either the dominant or submissive posturing. As long as you're firm in your neutral posturing, then they'll adjust to you. This is an important moment so that a dominant person knows that they can't push you around, which will make them have more respect for you because you're a strong person, and a submissive person will feel that you're treating them as an equal and will therefore have more respect for you because you're showing them respect.

Third: A Firm Grip

The reality is that we can't control whether our hands are clammy, but we can control whether our grip is firm. A clammy, limp hand communicates laziness, discomfort, and lack of confidence and strength. Instead, make your hand solid. Don't let your hand be crushed and don't crush the other person. Approach handshakes with your hand already partially squeezing an invisible hand, and you'll never get caught off-guard or give a wet fish handshake. You can always soften your handshake to match the other person's without crushing theirs.

Lastly: Set Your Shakes

For me, I do a single shake. Some people will go for two, some for three, some for far more than that. This is a delicate balance. In order to establish yourself as a confident and competent authority figure, you want to determine how many shakes there are ultimately, however also be conscious of how many shakes the other person is inclined to give.

There are a number of different personality types, and each one prefers a different way to shake hands. Some prefer them to be short and sweet, concise and pointed, a hard start and end to each up and down of the shake - these people are focused on getting things done. Some people prefer a more complex handshake, like the kind you'd do with a friend, and you'll often see them shake hands quicker and in smaller shakes - these people are more focused on making friends. Some people prefer a long handshake that is more like a wave, smooth and fluid - these people are more interested in connecting with others and value community over all else. Lastly, some people are very particular and a handshake should last for three distinct shakes, then end - these people care more about details and how things are done.

When it comes to building rapport, remember that like attracts like, and people tend to prefer those who are more like them, so it's helpful to match their handshake to the extent possible. I tend to prefer a single shake, so I go for that and if I notice the other person starting to lift for a second or third, I lead by getting ahead of their lift. This isn't completely necessary, but it can be a nice touch if you do it right. It can also be a terrible thing if you try to overpower them, so be cautious how you use this. Your goal is always a student's comfort so every interaction with you ends with them feeling better than when the interaction started.

Bonus: Secret Handshakes

I know I said lastly on the previous one, but this is too good for me not to share with you. It doesn't necessarily have to do with building rapport, but secret handshakes a great way to help build your community. Even now, as an adult, I still have different handshakes for different friend groups. I remember when I learned my first secret handshake as a kid - it made me feel like an official part of the group. Create a secret handshake and share it with your students! It's an awesome feeling seeing your students greet one another in a way that makes every single one of them feel at home, like they're where they belong.

Playfulness

Kids love to laugh. That's just a fact. When I say playfulness, I mean joking around with students to continue building rapport while at the same time keeping the serious tone in class so that kids don't get overly distracted. Adding elements of playfulness into your instruction will help keep students focused and organized since they have something to distract them from the boredom of standing still. They'll listen more readily because they don't want to miss a chance to laugh with everyone else.

Playfulness can come in many forms, whether it be relating a quick funny story in the middle of a class, or finding a funny example to get your point across, or being overly expressive with your movements and finding a comical way to say something. There are a thousand ways to be playful and most people have it in them naturally. As instructors, don't be afraid to use this playfulness to help teach kids the way they should go. Children should never lose their spirit of playfulness. As instructors, we should find every way to foster a child's playfulness by staying in touch with our own and using it as we teach them to build healthy habits that will develop them into successful adults.

Key Takeaways

- Give more high-fives! They build rapport and uplift moods.
- Handshake with a smiling face, vertical hand, and a firm grip.
- Be playful! When you're having fun, your students will want to learn what you have to teach.

SETTING EXPECTATIONS

Have you ever been in a situation where you aren't certain what's expected of you? Maybe you're asked to do something but not given the appropriate information to complete the task the way it's supposed to be. Maybe you've been driving in a new state and weren't sure if they had the same "turn on red" law as the state you're used to driving in. Maybe you've been volunteering and the person leading the event didn't give you a task, so you mindlessly wandered hoping somebody would give you something useful to do. The lack of expectation leaves you incapable of doing the job to your own satisfaction or the satisfaction of the person in charge. It also causes undue stress as you fear the judgment of those who under informed you for the job.

Lack of expectations can cause frustration, stress, and anxiety, and this is true for students also. There are behavioral expectations to set as well as expectations for whatever is being taught in class that day, and we should approach both similarly.

I've always said that it's important to treat kids with respect and to value their opinions. Not to act as if you value their opinions, but to truly value their opinions. I make it a point to ask my students for their opinions on various things throughout the year, regardless of age, whether it's a new class structure or an event we're setting up or how they liked the organization of an event or rules of a competition, etc.

Likewise, at the beginning of a class, as they do the standard warm-ups that start the first three minutes of every class (for consistency), I also explain the day's plan. This gives students a chance to mentally prepare for the day. If I tell them, "Today, we're working on acrobatics," versus, "Today, we're working on balance," they'll be prepared for what's to come. If there is a larger group than normal, I announce that to them: "It looks like we have a larger class than usual, so we're going to break into four groups today instead of our normal three," or something to that effect. The idea here is to communicate with them. When we show people respect, whether kids as young as four or adults well into their seventies, they'll return that respect.

The same goes for behavioral expectations in class. At AMP Academy, we have a set of rules on our wall that every student knows. The expectation has been set from the beginning that when a rule is broken, push-ups are given. When rules are followed, we always give praise as positive reinforcement. For instance, when classes start, I no longer have to say how to begin. At this point, even with our 4-year-olds, I invite the kids in for class and they automatically circle up and start with jumping jacks. Everytime I see that, I reinforce the message again, "Look at that, you guys are already hard at work without me even having to ask! I love it! I can tell we're going to get a lot done today! Great job!"

One hundred percent of setting expectations is good communication and consistency. Let students know exactly what's expected of them by giving specific praise when students perform a behavior you want repeated, and also being very specific about why you hand out push-ups or whatever disciplinary action you choose. Clear, concise, matter-of-fact, and friendly. "You know you're not supposed to climb on things while the instructor is explaining something, bud. Ten push-ups." And then move on without making a big deal out of it. Adding in the word "bud" or "buddy" or any other term of endearment is important to let the child know that you're not mad and you're not disciplining them because you don't like them - they just broke a rule and breaking rules have consequences. Everybody follows the same rules.

Set expectations early, be consistent, and you'll see awesome results.

Key Takeaways

- Set expectations early and your class will be more structured.
- Be specific as you praise students for following expectations.
- When a student knows what's expected, they'll be more conscious of doing it.

ASSIGNING RESPONSIBILITIES

Independence is the doorway to success, and responsibility is the key. Let's picture for a moment a family of four where both parents are at work when their children get home from school. When neither parent is present, who is responsible for the house and children while they're gone? The oldest child. I've personally seen this very scenario played out at least twice in my life, and it's common enough where it's become a stereotype seen on TV. The more familiar a child is with responsibility, the more comfortable that child will be when responsibility is given to them in adulthood, and the greater the responsibilities they'll be able to take on themselves. Many adults struggle with things like time management, finances, and priorities because we simply weren't given many responsibilities when we were growing up.

The most effective way to foster independence is to give students the opportunity to be exactly that. Students will become however you treat them. If we treat them like a failure, they're more likely to become a failure because it's become the expectation of them. They won't ever need to try hard, or even have the motivation to because they'll already expect to fail. I've met so many adults like this that it's greatly informed how I interact with children and how I treat them. If you demonstrate trust in your students and give them responsibilities, they're more likely to rise to the occasion so as not to disappoint you. That said, one of the most valuable things you can do for a child's future success is to teach them responsibility from a young age.

Start with something small. It doesn't have to be a huge responsibility at first, but it should be something significant. For instance, in martial arts, the student should be responsible for remembering their uniform - not their parents. Students know their uniform is required for class. They know there are consequences for not being in uniform. Parents don't have to run laps or do push-ups if the child forgets their uniform. The child does. So let the child be responsible for that. If students remember their uniform, they're rewarded by not being disciplined. If they forget their uniform, they might receive some kind of disciplinary action, like push-ups or burpees or something along those lines. Let students learn that their actions have consequences.

Similarly, every martial arts student should learn how to tie their own martial arts belt. It's part of the discipline of a martial art. When parents take the responsibility away from the child, the child is the one to suffer.

No parent wants to set their child up for failure, so instead set them up for success by teaching them how to do it and allowing them to do it themselves, or with minimal help as you walk them through it, not do it for them.

Another thing we do here at AMP Academy is ensure that our students check themselves in. We make it the child's responsibility to do it themselves, not their parents. To some parents of younger children, like 4-year-olds, this may seem like a silly policy. To those parents, I say it's a learning opportunity for the child and it's an important piece of keeping our classes organized here. The organization and focus in our Mini Ninja classes speak for themselves. We set expectations for our students, and they begin the moment a student walks through the door.

Our students are responsible for remembering their uniforms. They're responsible for checking into class to log attendance and ensure they have enough classes to be promoted to their next rank. Our students are responsible for paying attention in class to learn what's being taught. They're responsible for watching the instructor to see what's being said. By parents or instructors doing something as basic as checking a child in for class themselves, it sets the expectation that students don't have responsibilities while they're in class.

Remember that consistency is key. We give students responsibilities the moment they walk through the door so that they're primed to perform their more important responsibilities when they're in class - to focus, listen, learn, and work hard. Your responsibilities at any job happen the moment you walk into the facility. If you don't punch in, you don't get paid. If you don't focus and listen in meetings, you don't know what your job is and you don't do it. If you don't work hard, you won't be successful. Everything translates into adulthood.

Empower children for success by trusting that they have the capacity to do things themselves. Give kids responsibilities at a young age and you'll find them to be far more responsible in adolescence, high school, college, their careers, and their life.

Lastly, a major benefit to instructors teaching students about responsibility is that it alleviates pressure from parents. If a child knows they're responsible for their uniform and belt, then parents don't need to worry about it. The child learns that there are consequences for their actions, instead of being disciplined for something their parents did or didn't do, which can lead to something called Learned Helplessness that I'll share a study about later.

I know giving a child responsibilities sounds scary, but giving children responsibilities builds trust. It shows parents that their child can be trusted to accomplish certain things without needing us there to hold their hands. It shows kids that their parents trust them to make good decisions and contribute to the success of a particular family task. If you show a child you trust them, they will do everything in their power to prove that they deserve it.

Giving responsibilities creates trust. Trust creates Independence. Independence leads to success. Hold responsibilities away from a child, and they never grow. Give your students responsibilities and watch their abilities to shoulder more responsibilities grow as they become more experienced.

It can be tempting to just pick one person to be responsible for a greater task in a group because once somebody has proved themselves, it's just easier to continue trusting that person. However, it's our job to ensure that every child has the same opportunities to grow and become successful. Be sure to spread your trust out amongst all of your students through responsibility and give them all the opportunity for independence.

Key Takeaways

- Independence is the door to success. Responsibility is the key.
- Make students responsible for something they have to do daily.
- Give students responsibilities to help them grow.

MAKING AGREEMENTS WITH STUDENTS

In order to empower children for success, class organization and focus is a primary objective, and that can be difficult if you don't have this secret. When we hold birthday parties at AMP Academy, parents often say to me, "This group of kids is crazy - I don't know how you got them all to listen so well!" Somebody always asks if I was in the military or something else. Kids have followed direction for me my whole life, even before I was a formal instructor and ran my own classes. And I'm about to give you my secret. Are you ready for it?

Make an agreement with the students.

"How do you make an agreement with a 4-year-old?"

Kids are much smarter than people give them credit for. I once published a short story called "The Wax Man" from the perspective of an infant having his first interaction with a candle, where I intentionally used language that didn't match his perceived intellect from an adult's understanding. But here's the thing, children are far more sophisticated than adults think. Just because children don't have the vocabulary to express their thoughts and feelings doesn't mean they aren't experiencing the world in the same advanced way that we are.

Children don't have the same words or understanding of the world in terms of physics and science as adults, so we assume they aren't as intelligent. The reality is that they have the capacity to observe and analyze just as intricately as adults. Children's brains are constantly interpreting the world around them and making decisions based on the experiences they've had, limited though they may be. So, it's easy to make an agreement with a 4-year-old, as long as you help them to understand what's being asked of them. And it gets even easier the older they get.

Generally, people are good and people want to be considered good and viewed in a positive light. Since nobody likes being lied to, we generally try to be as honest as possible to remain in that positive light. Therefore, if you get a student to promise something, they will try to follow through for the sake of consistency. Sometimes they will forget, but that promise will remain in their unconscious mind and it will help dissuade them from doing something they aren't supposed to, sometimes even more so than if they'd been consciously thinking about it.

People wonder how I can maintain control of so many kids on my own, and this is the answer. With my regular students that I see every day, it's easy because the rules are posted and they see those rules enforced every day - expectations set and consistency. It's more challenging when there is a birthday party with a dozen or two brand new kids that don't know the expectations we have here at our school. This is why at every AMP Academy birthday party, one of the first things we do is sit down with the kids to make three agreements.

The first agreement is that they will listen to the instructor as they're teaching and refrain from hanging on things, jumping up and down, or interrupting. We give a quick reminder that there will be time for questions at the end of every explanation - again, setting expectations - so this helps kids to hold in their questions and comments for the appropriate time. After giving a brief explanation that this is for safety reasons, we then ask, "Do you all agree to Rule Number One?" Once every child gives a verbal agreement to this rule, we can move on.

The second and third agreements don't relate to keeping an organized class, so there's no need to share them.

Along with the first agreement, I determine whether the consequences need to be explained or not. If it looks like a pretty good group, I usually won't say anything until it becomes necessary. However, if a group seems rowdy at the start, part of the first agreement from the beginning includes a consequence for breaking the rules.

I might say something like, "So far you guys are doing a great job of listening, so I don't think we'll have to worry about this, but just so you know, the first time somebody breaks these rules, they get 10 push-ups. If they break the rule a second time, they get 25 push-ups. If they break it a third time, they'll have to sit out until I invite them back in, IF I decide to let them back in. Does anybody have any questions about that? Does everybody agree to that?"

There are a few things happening here and I'd like to share some statistics about communication before getting into it. Communication is broken into three main pieces: Words, Tonality, and Body Language. In this theory of communication, 7% of communication is verbal or the words that we say, 38% is the tonality or how we say it, and 55% is nonverbal body language or what our bodies are saying beyond our words. This is why text messages and emails can be so challenging sometimes - because we only see the 7% that's verbal. I can say the same sentence a hundred different ways and each will make you feel differently about what I've said.

Now, back to the agreement of Rule Number One and its consequences. Notice how I start by assuming the best of them. I start by saying that they're doing a great job of listening, reinforcing from the beginning that listening is the expectation. The next part about them having to do push-ups I mention casually as if I don't expect to have to actually give out push-ups, thus setting the expectation once again that they'll do what they're supposed to and not need to be disciplined for breaking a rule. And the last part, I make super exaggerated faces as if it's the greatest crime they could commit, then I drop back into my light tone with a smile on my face as I ask if everybody understands and agrees to the rule. Having them agree to the rule verbally and not moving on until they've all agreed verbally reinforces the expectation yet again and the level of seriousness despite the playfulness in my tone.

Doing this has proven effective at keeping large groups of inexperienced students very organized and rarely do push-ups get dealt, much less the sitting out part. The most important thing, however - which we'll talk about more in the chapter on Reinforcing VS. Disciplining - is to follow up on any agreement you make. If you expect kids to stick to an agreement, you have to stick to it also. If you expect the kids to follow the rules you put in place, you have to follow them too. If a child agrees to not climb while you're talking or they'll get push-ups, and then they climb while you're talking, you're obligated to give that child push-ups, otherwise it tells the whole class that your word is worthless, and your class will disintegrate. Rules mean nothing without follow-through.

Following through on agreements is vital to helping children develop a sense of responsibility for a successful life. I remember when I would do something wrong as a kid and my mom used to take TV away. She usually took it away for a reasonable amount of time, like three days, or a week. One day, though, she said she'd take it away from us for a month.

I don't remember what it was for, but I was horrified. What I do know is that I ended up doing that thing and lost TV for a month, but my mom never planned to actually follow through on it. She was smart, though. Rather than letting the grounding fall apart, she gave me the opportunity to earn my TV privileges back. Through chores, good behavior, and doing all my homework, I was able to reduce my sentence from one month to only four days without TV. In retrospect, I see what she did. She taught us that working hard would be rewarded, and even if we made a mistake along the way, we could still pull ourselves out of it if we did the right thing.

I've seen other parents say no TV for a month, and then their child is watching TV that very night. This is the worst thing you can do. It breaks the agreement. It teaches children that their parents can't be trusted and that there are no consequences for their actions. That's dangerous to teach a child, especially if you want them to follow rules. Children need accountability. It's not about punishing for bad behavior - it's about ensuring future success.

The best thing we can do is keep control of our anger and frustration. Believe it or not, there is a right way to discipline a child, and it can be done very calmly and without any animosity. I'll go over the 3 Rules for Disciplining Correctly in the chapter on Reinforcing VS. Disciplining, after discussing the four types of parenting styles and which is most effective. For now, however, suffice it to say that creating agreements with your students and being consistent will create an organized class full of children geared toward successful futures.

Key Takeaways

- Set expectations and consequences early and have students agree to the rules. Agreement will hold them at a subconscious level.
- Keep your promises. If you say you're going to do something, do it. It builds trust, respect, and discipline.
- Always remain in control. Never let anger take over.

BEING OMNISCIENT AND OMNIPRESENT

Keeping classes organized will help your students form successful habits, so I recommend learning some techniques for appearing omniscient and omnipresent when working with groups of kids. I use the idea of omniscience and omnipresence somewhat jokingly, but this is extraordinarily useful when teaching larger groups of kids. Omniscience means "knowing everything" and omnipresence means "being everywhere," and it's helpful for an instructor to appear as both. Instructors should always be paying attention to their students, no matter where they are or what they're doing. AMP Academy in Fall River, MA is 9,000 square feet, and when I'm the only instructor with 20 to 30 kids in a class, it's natural for students to expect that I can't have my eyes on them at all times.\

This comfort in knowing instructors don't have eyes in the back of their heads can lead some students to not work as hard or to just play around instead of doing the task given. I handle this based on the findings of the "Hawthorne Effect" - also known as the "Observer Effect" - which, fascinatingly, wasn't the actual subject of the study that ended up finding it.

Between 1924 and 1932, a series of studies took place at the Hawthorne Works factory in Illinois to determine whether lighting, cleanliness, relocated workstation, and a number of other variables affected productivity. When studying the results in 1958, Henry A. Landsberger found that productivity dropped after the experiments stopped. Landsberger's interpretation of this was that productivity increases when a worker is actively being observed.

I'm sure we've all felt the pressure of having a supervisor in the same room as you work on a given task. This can be stressful, but it often results in eustress as opposed to distress. Eustress is a positive stress that gets our brains firing on all cylinders. It helps us focus and therefore work more efficiently. As instructors, we can use this to our advantage also to keep kids on a path to success.

When I have larger classes, I break them into more groups so students get a good amount of time on each obstacle. What that means is that I have more places to keep my eyes on. When I have 30 kids broken up into six groups spread out over 9,000 square feet, there are a few tricks we can use to keep students engaged, working hard, and doing their best, while also letting observers know that you're watching everybody, even if you're not within arm's reach.

The first trick is to always position yourself so that you can see every station. You should be able to see at least part of every station from wherever you stand. Avoid putting your back to any group of students. If you're walking, keep your head on a swivel, looking behind you, around you, in front of you, up and down, making sure that you see everything.

The second thing is to make sure you know students' names. If you aren't great at remembering names, I'll have advice for that closer to the end of this chapter. Remembering names is important. Very important. I can't reiterate enough how important this is. Knowing all students' names is important for pulling off the whole omniscience and omnipresence thing. If I'm spotting Ryan on an obstacle and I yell from 40 feet away saying, "Keep that chest up, Lucy! Come on, Tommy, you've got this, man! Emily, eyes on the obstacle! Remember, looking down means you're looking for a way to fall. You've gotta keep your eyes on what you're doing or you've already given up," it communicates to everybody that I'm paying attention to them.

Every time a person hears their own name, they're going to work harder because they know you're watching. Every time they hear the name of somebody in their line, it reinforces that your eyes are going to be on them too. Every time a parent hears you call their child's name and give advice from across the room, they know that their child is important to you even if you aren't standing right beside them.

Tips for Remembering Names:

Tip 1: See their name written out.

Tip 2: Say their name out-loud.

Tip 3: Identify something unique about them.

Tip 4: Thank them by repeating their name.

Tip 5: Use their name often.

Bonus Tip: Ask a second time.

Your voice should be a constant stream of feedback and support. Don't forget to laugh and make jokes as you lead a class to keep the pressure off. Playfulness is huge when it comes to high-stress activities. Remember the lessons on building rapport - students are more likely to work hard if they have a good relationship with you than if they don't.

Knowing that you're watching will keep students engaged and productivity up. Your constant presence and activity in class will keep students focused and working hard, which will build positive habits, like a strong work ethic, that will propel them toward success.

Remembering Names

We've already established how important it is to remember names for the organization of your class and for building rapport. Another comment I get at birthday parties I run is, "Wow, I have no idea how you remembered so many kids' names that you just met today!"

Is it a talent? A gift?

Nope. It's all technique.

If you aren't great at remembering names, no problem! Here are a few tips and tricks that I use to help me remember names, and they can help you too.

Tip 1: See Their Name Written Out. This is probably the most useful thing for me because I'm a Visual Learner - we'll get more into the details of what that means later, but for now it essentially means that I learn and remember things better when I see them. If you have a roster or a printed waiver or an online check-in screen that you can look at, take advantage of it!

Tip 2: Say Their Name Out Loud. I take attendance at every birthday party and it's a huge help for remembering names. I get to see the name written out as I say it and then I get to associate the name with a child raising their hand. How the child raises their hand also offers valuable insights into how that child can best be helped in that class - whether they sit up tall and raise it high or stay hunched over and just

57

raise their hand at the wrist - but I digress. When taking attendance, if the child has a unique name or one that you aren't sure how to pronounce, don't be embarrassed to read it out completely wrong. Make it a point to ask them after you butcher the name if you were anywhere close. Go out of your way to ask how to pronounce their name the right way. This will demonstrate to that person and to everybody in the group that details are important to you, that their identity is important to you, and that their comfort and happiness is important to you. Once you have the pronunciation correct, you can move on.

Tip 3: Identify Something Unique About Them. Pick something about them that sticks out to you. Maybe they're the only student with a ponytail. Maybe they have super light blonde hair. Maybe their hair makes them look like an anime character. Maybe they're wearing a Star Wars shirt or an obscure shirt that you get the reference to. Maybe they have freckles or a bowl cut or a gap in their teeth or curly hair. Pick something about them and say their name in your mind as you look at it. This associates that child's name with a specific feature. If you can't remember their name by looking at them, look at that prominent feature that you associated their name with, and the name will pop back into your head like magic.

Tip 4: Thank Them by Name. Repeat their name again by thanking them for raising their hand. This does double work. It shows the student respect because you're thanking them, which is great for building rapport and ensuring that they'll show you respect for the rest of their time with you, and it allows you to get your third time saying their name: once when you read it, once when you said it in your head to associate their name with something about them, and a third time when you thanked them for identifying themselves and helping you remember their name.

The Magic of Three

Why is saying their name three times important?

- The most basic form of memorization is repetition.
- We're used to it from studying in school.
- Three repetitions is the minimum recommendation.
- Try saying it with a unique tone or sound to help remember better.

Fun Fact:

This is even more true if you're an Auditory Learner - we'll discuss this more in a later chapter, but it basically means that you learn best by listening.

Tip 5: Use Their Name Often. It may seem annoying, and it very well might be annoying, but if you want to avoid forgetting somebody's name, say it often. In NLP, it's commonly said that a person's own name is the sweetest sound to their ears. In fact, Andy from *The Office* did this when he first met his new boss, Michael Scott, for this exact reason.

Saying somebody's name in conversation can actually cause that person to like you more because you're demonstrating that you care enough about them to remember their name. The more you say a name, the more solid it becomes in your mind and the easier it is for you to remember later when you need it.

Bonus Tip: Just Ask Again. It's okay to ask again. It doesn't make you look bad. People worry somebody will be upset if you forgot their name the first time, but the reality is that people instead see that it's important enough to you that you're going out of your way to try to remember it by asking a second time. Use it as a way to build rapport yet again.

Remember, the more a person sees that you respect them, the more they'll respect you, which means they'll be more open to the positive influences you can contribute to their success.

Key Takeaways

- An organized class builds successful habits, like focus, self-control, discipline, and strong work ethic.
- Remembering names and calling advice from afar gives the illusion of omnipresence.
- Your voice should be a steady stream, always giving feedback and support. Let students know you care by paying attention to them.

PARENTING STYLES

As I mentioned at the beginning of this book, I consider coaching, teaching, instructing, and working with kids in general to be form of temporary or supplementary parenting, meaning we have the opportunity and the obligation to instill in our students the ability to recognize good from bad and right from wrong in a way that strengthens them as people. As an instructor, I recommend reading some books on parenting - there are always a few useful tips that you can use to strengthen your interactions with students. This chapter will give a basic understanding of the four primary parenting styles as identified by developmental psychologist Diana Baumrind of the University of California at Berkeley in the 1960's, and we'll briefly discuss the advantages and disadvantages of each according to her research.

The four parenting styles are Authoritarian, Authoritative, Permissive, and Uninvolved. These parenting styles are defined by two primary traits: Warmth and Control. Warmth refers to the affection a parent shows toward their child, such as hugging, supporting, encouraging, etc. Control refers to the rules a parent places on their children, such as curfews, academic expectations, behavioral expectations, etc. Each major parenting style breaks down as follows:

- Authoritarian - Low Warmth; High Control
- Authoritative - High Warmth; High Control
- Permissive - High Warmth; Low Control
- Uninvolved - Low Warmth; Low Control

As you can imagine from reading even the most basic breakdown of these parenting types, it's clear that the best form of parenting is one that is high in Warmth and high in Control. Thus, according to research, the Authoritative parenting style is the kind that will best prepare a child for their successful futures, both in dealing with authority figures and subordinates as well as in their personal relationships. The four styles of parenting can apply to how instructors interact with our students also, so be sure not to gloss over this part if you aren't a parent.

DISCLAIMER: Before reading on, let me make clear that I'm using caricatures and general statements in this section below to give you a basic understanding of the four parenting styles. Using extreme examples makes it easier to see the differences between each parenting style. These examples are generalizations and there are always examples where a child may grow up differently under each parenting style than the extreme examples I'm using below. These caricatures and generalizations are intended to be illustrative only to help you understand the importance of how we interact with children and the potential impact we can have on them.

What Does Uninvolved Parenting Look Like?

This is by far the worst and most dangerous style of parenting, and frankly the one that breaks my heart most to know that some children grow under. Uninvolved Parenting is low in warmth and low in control.

On the warmth side of things, these are the parents who don't hug their children or say "I love you," who treat them like an annoyance and an obligation rather than a gift and a privilege. Uninvolved parents don't praise their child for accomplishments or support them through failure. They often snap at their kids for asking for help with homework. Parents like this might put their kids in front of a video game or TV for hours just so they don't have to interact with them.

On the control side of things, these types of parents don't care what their children do or whether their sub-13-year-old stays out late into the night and early into the morning hours. It doesn't matter to them if their kids do their homework or keep their room clean. Uninvolved parents take no responsibility for the person they're creating.

Children under this parenting style can grow up without a sense of right or wrong. Or worse, they may not care what's right or wrong.

These children have nobody who shows them love or expresses any attachment to them, and that can cause them to become calloused individuals who don't care about the feelings or wellbeing of others. This can lead to violence towards others or a complete indifference to others' struggles. These types of people might not understand that they can't just do whatever they want with no ramifications for their actions. This parenting style is almost certain to create a child who will only harm society and the community in which they live.

What Does Permissive Parenting Look Like?

We've all seen parents like this, the kind of parent who just wants to be their child's friend. Permissive parents don't want to control their child because they want their child to like them. They're the parents who coddle their child. A "Helicopter Parent" might be a term you hear for a parent like this. They show intense warmth and help their child do everything, never letting their child make mistakes so they can learn on their own. It's the parent at the playground who carries a child across the monkey bars, then praises the child for making it across, even though the child didn't have any weight on their arms and did no real work.

When the child does invariably do something wrong, these are the parents that might say, "My child would never do that," or they'd blame somebody else for making their child react in that way. These parents are the type to get upset when another parent tells their child not to do something, regardless of how calm and rational the other parent may have spoken. This type of parent might brush off something as just "kids being kids," never realizing the greater impact that not holding their child accountable will have on their child's future. Permissive parents might even blame a teacher for their child failing a class rather than recognizing that their child might not have put in the work.

Kids raised this way can grow up dependent on their parents, never taking responsibility for anything because their parents always take care of it for them. Their parents pay for everything, even when their kids go to college, and they never learn to work hard or be responsible. Permissive parenting, in extreme cases, can lead children to fall in with the wrong crowd, become partiers, and sometimes fall deep into drugs.

What Does Authoritarian Parenting Look Like?

This seems to have been the most common type of parenting style from fathers in the early 1900's. At least, it's the type of fatherly parenting seen most commonly on popular 80's and 90's TV shows. It wasn't until the last thirty or forty years where this type of parenting shifted to a larger number of fathers showing their children more warmth.

In this parenting style, parents are high in control, which means that children grow up with a respect that might also just be fear. Children live every day knowing that if they do something wrong, they'll be disciplined for it, whether with a physical form of discipline such as a spanking, verbal abuse such as being called stupid or useless, or a grounding form of discipline where TV, video games, or friends are witheld for a set time. In ideal situations, this prevents children from making bad decisions in hopes of avoiding negative repercussions.

In extreme cases of Authoritarian Parenting, when there's irrationally high control with irrationally low warmth, parents yell at kids for making too much noise while playing, or react overdramatically for some other small reason. This is a caricature we often see in movies, particularly when there is an alcoholic parent who yells and throws things at their kids all the time. Obviously, this more extreme form of Authoritarian Parenting is more like abuse than parenting, and kids who grow up this way need a mentor high in warmth more than anybody.

This parenting style is low in warmth, usually exemplified by parents who don't tell their children, "I love you," or who don't hug their kids or tuck their kids in at night, who don't have family meals with their children, etc. Nowadays, it's common for people to joke about a bully's parents not hugging them when they were little. People make light of it, but it can have truly traumatic effects. Bullying is only one example. In extreme cases, parenting like this can lead to violent behavior in adults, including domestic abuse and mass violence.

What Does Authoritative Parenting Look Like?

Of course, I saved the scientifically evidenced best for last. Authoritative Parenting is high in warmth and high in control. These parents go out of their way to spend time with their children, be involved in their lives, play with them, know what's going on, and help with homework. These parents are actively involved in their children's lives, and thus children feel that warmth because they see it every day. These parents cheer their kids on when they're trying something new, encouraging them to push past all their failures.

These parents are also high in control, setting curfews and high academic expectations, giving children responsibilities like chores and limited freedoms. Authoritative parents allow kids to fail and learn from their mistakes to keep growing. These parents also discipline their children appropriately when necessary. If a child doesn't do their homework, they might not get dessert. If they make a scene in a grocery store, they might not get to go to the playground.

Children of Authoritative parents are typically more successful than those of other parenting styles due to the higher level of parental involvement and encouragement. This style of parenting creates more independent children because these parents afford their children more trust, which is earned during the parent's increased involvement in a child's life. These parents encourage children to learn from their failures until they succeed, building their confidence and self-esteem. These children grow up feeling loved and showing love, and this provides the perfect combination for an emotionally and psychologically healthy child geared toward success.

According to Baumrind's Research	
Typically, children raised by each of the following parenting styles demonstrate:	
Authoritarian • Less independence • Lower academic success • Low self-esteem & insecurity • Behavioral problems • Poor social skills • Poor mental health • Tendencies for drug abuse	**Authoritative** • More independence • High academic success • High self-esteem & confidence • Greater respect for authority • Better social skills • Better mental health • Less violent tendencies
Permissive • Less self-control & self-restraint • Egocentricity and selfishness • Sense of entitlement • Poor interpersonal relationships • Poor social interactions	**Uninvolved** • Impulsivity • Emotional outbursts (typically anger) • Rule-breaking & delinquency • Tendencies for drug abuse & addiction • Suicidal tendencies in youths

Closing Thoughts on Parenting Styles

With any parenting style, there are pros and cons, and with every parenting style a child can grow up to be a healthy adult with the proper balance. Even the preferred method of Authoritative Parenting can have negative repercussions if a parent is overly warm or overly controlling.

A parental figure, including us as temporary or supplementary parents, needs to find the right balance of warmth and control.

I cannot overstate the importance of being aware of how you're treating students and how your interactions with them, both affectionately and disciplinarily, can and will affect their entire lives. There will always be children that are difficult to work with. There will always be children that refuse to listen to you no matter how hard you try. Remember that these are the kids with Uninvolved or Permissive parents. These are the kids that need your help the most, the ones that need your patience most, that need your warmth most, and your control most. These are the kids with the highest risk of ending up on a dangerous path that can lead to them hurting themselves or others, emotionally or physically.

When you have these students, pay them the most attention, and make sure it's the right kind of attention. Praise them when they behave the way they're supposed to behave. Discipline them appropriately when they behave in a way they aren't supposed to behave. Do not let kids get away with things because you don't feel like dealing with it or because you don't think you'll have an effect. Half the time children behave poorly, it's because they're craving attention. Don't let them slip through the cracks.

If you can show a child warmth and affection even as you demonstrate control through discipline, students will appreciate you more than you could imagine. When you discipline a child affectionately to help them become a better person, you demonstrate care. You demonstrate that they matter. You wouldn't do it if you didn't care. You have a unique opportunity every single day to change a child's life for the better. Be an authoritative instructor and always demonstrate warmth to your students, even in discipline.

Key Takeaways

- Students who are the worst behaved are the students hurting most inside. These are the students who need us the most.
- Demonstrate warmth and control equally toward students for the most positive impact on success.
- Correcting poor behavior demonstrates both warmth and affection when done right.

REINFORCING VS. DISCIPLINING

Let's get this out of the way early - there is merit to both reinforcement and disciplinary action. It's proven that reinforcement is better for long-term behavioral changes, while disciplinary action can be effective for short-term changes. Reward is always the better option, though disciplinary action has its place when done correctly, and I can't overemphasize this point enough. After all, "You catch more flies with honey than you do with vinegar."

So when is it appropriate to reinforce or to discipline? In order to better understand this, I'd like to first give a short history lesson and to define a few things. Edward Thorndike first put forward the "Law of Effect" in 1905, which essentially stated that behaviors leading to pleasant consequences are likely to be repeated, while behaviors leading to unpleasant consequences are likely to be reduced or stopped. Burrhus Fredric Skinner further studied this effect in the 1930's, when he elaborated on the idea of positive reinforcement in developing the theory of Operant Conditioning, which Skinner coined in his 1938 publication

"The Behavior of Organisms."

In Operant Conditioning, there are two types of desired results, which are achieved using four types of consequences:

Results:

1. Repeat Behavior (Reinforcement)

2. Eliminate Behavior (Punishment)

Consequences:

1. Positive Reinforcement

2. Negative Reinforcement

3. Positive Punishment

4. Negative Punishment

I use the word "punishment" only to properly and accurately explain Operant Conditioning. I do however make an important distinction between "punishment" and "discipline" or "disciplinary actions." In everyday speech, "punishment" has the connotation of destructive intent to harm somebody as payback, whereas "discipline" and "disciplinary action" is done with the constructive intent to educate and inform to modify behavior. No instructor should ever seek to "punish" a student. Appropriate disciplinary action is acceptable to modify behavior only so long as they follow the 3 Rules for Disciplining Correctly listed in this chapter.

In the context of Operant Conditioning, consider Positive and Negative mathematically rather than in terms of good and bad or optimism and pessimism. Positive literally means something being added or given, while negative literally means something being subtracted or removed. (See the operant conditioning chart on the next page.)

That means that Positive Reinforcement is the idea of giving something desired in order for them to repeat a behavior. An example of this is rewarding a child with ice cream after they get a good grade. The pleasant consequence of ice cream is given in order to encourage hard work and study so they continue to get good grades. Deeming a child "Star of the Day" for great focus is another example of this. The pleasant consequence of prestige, positive attention from peers, and pride of parents by being the "Star of the Day" is given to inspire continued great focus in class in hopes of receiving "Star of the Day" for the next class and future classes.

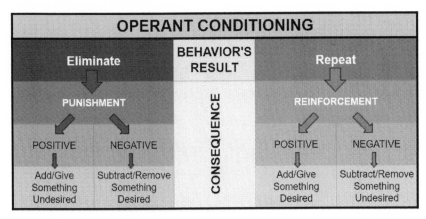

Negative Reinforcement, then, is the idea of removing something to encourage repeat behavior. An example of Negative Reinforcement might be rewarding somebody by not making them take a final if they received A's on all of their tests throughout the semester. The reward of not having to study or take a final is used to encourage students to do well throughout the rest of the semester. Another example is what my mom did with my TV privileges when I was little. She used Negative Punishment to discipline me by taking TV privileges for a month, then subtracted time to reward my good behavior. In this instance, the reward of not having to wait a month to watch TV was a pleasant consequence that caused me to repeat the modified behavior.

By this same logic, Positive Punishment or discipline is when an unpleasant consequence is given to eliminate a behavior. Detention for starting a fight or failing a test is an example of Positive Punishment. The unpleasant consequence of detention is given to eliminate fighting or poor grades in the future. Push-ups for breaking a rule is another example, where push-ups are the unpleasant consequence and rule breaking is the behavior to be eliminated.

Lastly, Negative Punishment or discipline refers to removal of something to eliminate a behavior. Parents sending their child to bed without dessert, or take away TV privileges for a week are examples of this. Taking away TV is the unpleasant consequence intended to eliminate whatever behavior earned that disciplinary action. In my classes, I sometimes take away a minute or two or three of playtime for breaking rules, based on how severe the rulebreaking was, of course. The unpleasant experience of not being able to play with their friends helps to eliminate whatever behavior lost them that time.

Understanding the benefits and ramifications of both forms of Reinforcement and Punishment or disciplinary action and the intensity with which you administer them will be instrumental in helping children build good habits for a successful future.

3 RULES FOR DISCIPLINING CORRECTLY

Let me be clear that I do not condone physical violence as a disciplinary action. When I was a child, I was disciplined with spanking, as my parents were disciplined with spanking by their parents, though I fortunately never had to go out and pick my own switch. I don't resent my parents for raising me and disciplining me the way they did - in fact, as I said before, I attribute much of my success to the way they raised me. They did their best with me and my brother after having kids at a young age and with little life experience. I love them both very much and I'm thankful every day for how they raised us. In my adulthood, knowing what I know and doing what I do as a profession, I can see the flaws in their actions, but I also understand their intent and have come to appreciate the things they did right also. Their process was great, though their method was not ideal.

Now, let's get into the rules.

Rule #1: All disciplinary actions given *__must__* match the crime.

If a child eats a cookie when you never said they couldn't, is that the same as them eating a cookie when you already told them no? Are either of those the same as coming home from a friend's house an hour later than promised? How about stealing a videogame from Walmart? Are any of those the same as committing violence against somebody?

Obviously, each of those scenarios require vastly different disciplinary actions, though they all require some form. The first might just call for a conversation because maybe the child didn't know they weren't supposed to eat the cookie. A child consciously defying you, however, would call for a greater disciplinary action.

Applying a greater disciplinary action for a lesser crime makes you dangerously unpredictable to a child. Taking video games away for a week because they ate a cookie without being told they couldn't is overkill. Children will often say that it's not fair, because it doesn't make sense. Taking video games away for a week does match the crime of them stealing a videogame, though, and if a child claims that isn't fair, then a calm, logical conversation about why that was the disciplinary action is the best tactic.

If you really want to help a student make better decisions in their lives that will ultimately lead to their success, they have to understand. Never use the Authoritarian parent's favorite phrase, "Because I said so." Anytime you administer a disciplinary action, no matter the severity, if a child questions the fairness or the reason, it's best to explain it to them so they can understand the rules better. Growth comes through understanding. If your goal is modified behavior for future success, and it always should be, then helping children understand the why of something is the only way to ensure a positive change.

Rule #2: All disciplinary actions _must_ be followed through.

I mentioned this briefly in the chapter on Making Agreements with Students, and while none of these rules works on their own, this one might be the most important. If a child steals a videogame and you take videogames away from them for a week, but then you forget and let them play videogames tomorrow, you've taught them that the crime wasn't serious. By not following through, it tells students they can repeat the bad behavior, which sets them on a dangerous path for the future. Following through is necessary for students to recognize that there are consequences for their actions.

Along with that, by doling out a disciplinary action and not following through, it teaches students that your disciplinary actions are irrational and unjust. It teaches them that you're not reliable and they can't trust your word. Demonstrating trustworthiness is important for building relationships with students. Students want to know they can trust you. If you say you won't get mad or they won't get in trouble if they admit something, they want to know you're safe to talk to. This is the basis of being a person of honor, and it's non-negotiable if you want to make the greatest impact possible on your students.

As a bonus tip, never suggest a disciplinary action you aren't willing to commit to. I made that mistake when I first started teaching my own classes, and I'd like to share this story with you as a cautionary tale. Don't make the mistake that I did. I had a small class with an unruly 8-year-old refusing to stay in line, pushing others, and running around while I was trying to explain an obstacle. After about 15 minutes of patience and using all the techniques I'd learned up to that point, certain that it would get him to listen, I said, "If you don't start following the rules, bud, you're not gonna be allowed to take classes here anymore."

I shouldn't have said that, because he didn't start following the rules, and I had to follow through, otherwise he and my other students in class would have learned that I don't mean what I say and they don't have to listen to me. So, because I didn't have the presence of mind to be rational and put forth a disciplinary action that I was okay following through on, I unfortunately had to ban that student. It's unfortunate because, as you'll see me say a lot throughout this book, it's the toughest students that need us the most, and I took myself out of his life when I should have been there to help him.

As a brief addendum to that story, I reached out to the student two years later to explain my mistake and to apologize. Some may wonder why apologize to a 10-year-old child about something that happened when he was 8, but another thing that I'll say a thousand times in this book is that I believe in respecting every single person, whether they're four years old or a hundred. Everybody deserves respect. He may have been disrespectful to me, but I was unfair to him and it limited my ability to be in his life to help him form successful habits.

I tell this story as a warning. Never threaten to take something away permanently. You absolutely must follow through on all disciplinary actions given. Thus, you absolutely must be willing to follow through on all the disciplinary actions given. When deciding what disciplinary action is suitable, first ensure that you're willing to deal with the consequences of it yourself.

Rule #3: All disciplinary actions *must* be followed with a chance to make amends.

It's best to not end an interaction by administering a disciplinary action. Remember that disciplinary actions are only good for short-term changes. It might help immediately, but it's unlikely that corrected behavior will carry into future classes unless you end the interaction with a reward. In an instance where a student receives push-ups, make it a point to praise them in the next five minutes if they don't repeat the behavior that earned the push-ups.

If a student loses playtime at the end of class, when I sit down with them to discuss why they lost playtime, they always have a chance to earn some of that playtime back if they're focused during our conversation and can identify what led them to losing time in the first

79

place. This chance for them to make up for their bad behavior is your chance to reward them and thus provide the positive reinforcement that will lead to long-term modification of their behavior.

Remember that when you give a student the opportunity to be the type of person they want to be, when you give them the benefit of the doubt and assume their best intentions, it gives them an opportunity to self-monitor and change for the better. People become how you treat them. If you treat children like they aren't valuable, they will start to believe that they aren't and act like they aren't. If a student has the chance to be the person they want to be because you've kept that option open with the way you treat them, they are far more likely to be successful.

This is further exemplified by the infamous "Monster Study" performed by Wendell Johnson in 1939 at the University of Iowa. During this aptly named experiment, dubbed so by Johnson's colleagues for the inhumanity of it, Johnson took 22 orphan children with speech impediments and praised half of them for their fluency as they progressed through speech therapy, criticizing and belittling the other half for every error they made, no matter how minor. The positive speech therapy led to significant growth, while the negative speech therapy resulted in many negative psychological effects and left some participants with lifelong speech problems.

We absolutely must be positive influences on our students' lives. It is both morally and ethically wrong for anybody to ever "take their day out" on a child, whose mind is so sensitive and malleable. The effects of such an interaction can last long into adulthood and can affect that person's personal and professional relationships for the rest of their life. Remember that it's often the children who are most frustrating to us that need us the most. We have both the opportunity and the responsibility to give them a fair chance in life by treating them in the way that is most conducive to their future success.

CLOSING THOUGHTS

When considering the question of disciplinary action and reinforcement, particularly when working with groups, we can look back to the Bobo Doll Experiment by Albert Bandura detailed in the chapter on Role Modeling, Ethics, & Morals. This experiment also indicated that children are just as likely to respond to Observational Conditioning as they are to Operant Conditioning. Observational Conditioning simply refers to the idea of a child witnessing somebody else being rewarded or disciplined for good or bad behavior and learning a lesson from that experience without having experienced the reward or disciplinary action themselves.

A lighthearted example of this, for fans of The Office, is the episode where Jim, after being promoted to co-manager, is struggling with his coworkers not respecting his new position. This is exemplified by Ryan

- "the temp" - playing Tetris while shirking a job that Jim had asked him to do. Jim took the opportunity to "make an example" of Ryan. He called the attention of the whole office as he announced Ryan's relocation to a brand new office - inside a tiny storage closet. Ryan tried to apologize and get out of the disciplinary action, but Jim was a man of his word and followed through. From then on, the office respected him as an authority figure.

Now, obviously I'm not suggesting locking a child in a closet or "making an example" out of a child. Still, there's a lesson to be learned. If you're having trouble with a group of students believing you're a person of your word, the best course is to stick to your word. Once children recognize that you're serious when you say something, they'll take you more seriously, and you'll immediately recognize better organization and listening skills in your classes.

No form of discipline should be given in anger as a way to punish a child. Punishment seeks to harm, while discipline seeks to educate. A positive attitude and positive intentions should always be maintained when disciplining students to demonstrate your sincerity.

Use Observational Conditioning to your advantage, but never be cruel. Always use the guidelines above for any disciplinary actions. Remember that disciplinary action is a short-term solution meant only to handle an immediate behavior issue, while reinforcement is always a more effective tool for long-term changes in behavior. Consistency is key.

Key Takeaways

- Disciplinary action is good for immediate behavior modification.
- Reinforcement is always the better choice for long-term behavior modification.
- Remember the 3 Rules for Disciplining Correctly
  - All disciplinary actions given *must* fit the crime.
  - All disciplinary actions given *must* be followed through.
  - All disciplinary actions given *must* be followed with a chance to make amends.

USING SOCIAL PROOF

Social proof is the phenomenon that occurs when we see somebody doing something and thus are more inclined to do so also, and it's your ally when it comes to creating good habits for students to have success in their lives. It directly relates to conformity and our desire to fit in. It makes everybody face the same direction in an elevator. If you walked into an elevator full of people facing the back of the elevator, would you continue facing the front? Or would you face the rear also, assuming that the rest of the passengers knew something that you didn't.

Social proof is also used in sales and marketing, particularly in commercials. Infomercials use testimonials as their social proof, while many cologne and shaving cream advertisements demonstrate that men are more attractive when wearing a particular scent or using a specific shaving cream. It works as a sales tactic toward men because it addresses the psychological needs in Maslow's Hierarchy of Needs, the need for belongingness and love, intimate relationships and friendships. When there's evidence that wearing a certain cologne brings people their ideal relationship, we're subconsciously more interested in that cologne.

There are a number of fascinating experiments that demonstrate social proof and its effectiveness in our lives, though for the sake of brevity, I'll mention only two. A 2015 episode of "Brain Games" aired on National Geographic demonstrating social proof in an unbelievable and humorous way. In the scene, 10 people sat in a waiting room. Nine were accomplices, while the tenth was the unassuming subject of the experiment. For the experiment, the accomplices were instructed to stand up briefly every time they heard a beeping noise to see if the subject would conform to the behavior. After only three beeps, the subject began to stand up at the sound of the beep. One by one, each accomplice was called out of the room until only the subject remained. At the sound of the beep, can you guess what she did?

That's right, even after everyone else had left the room, the subject continued to stand up at the sound of the beep. The show decided to see if the trend would continue, so they sent in another unassuming subject. Subject Two, after the second beep, asked Subject One why she was standing up. She told him, "I don't know. Everybody else was, so I thought I was supposed to." At the sound of the next beep, Subject Two stood also. As the experimenters sent in more and more subjects, they all began to conform to the same beep-stand pattern despite not understanding why they were behaving this way.

In another experiment, known as the Asch Conformity Experiments, which took place significantly earlier in the 1950's and have been a foundational piece in conformity and peer pressure research, Solomon Asch researched conformity in perception. Eight college-aged men participated in the experiment, seven of which were accomplices, while the eighth was an unassuming subject. Each participant saw a card with a line on it, and then were asked to pair that line with its duplicate on a card that had three clearly differently-sized lines, each labeled A, B, or C. Eighteen (18) trials of this experiment took place, twelve (12) of which the accomplices gave intentionally incorrect answers with varying outcomes from each.

The false participants were asked first which line matched the original card, at which point they all, one-by-one, said a line that was very obviously not the same length as the original card. The subject was always the last to answer the questions. Of the twelve critical trials where the accomplices gave incorrect responses, when all the numbers were tallied up, 5% of the subjects conformed to the accomplices' answers despite them being obviously wrong, 25% refused to conform regardless of what the accomplices said, and 75% of the subjects gave at least one incorrect response, thus demonstrating the importance of fitting in and having a sense of belonging.

So what does this mean for us and how can we take advantage of social proof ethically to help our students remain focused in classes and develop a strong work ethic for success?

One of my favorite things to do, particularly with younger children, is the combination of social proof with positive reinforcement. In classes, I have a digital clock on the wall that counts down the seconds. My students know that our classes begin punctually, so my students huddle at the edge of the mat, counting down the seconds until class begins. The moment the clock strikes the hour, my students flood into the space and immediately begin with jumping jacks. '

If there is a new student in class, they'll typically get right to work, following the social proof of the students around them, but sometimes they do need a bit of prompting, and that's where the positive reinforcement comes in. A quick, "Look at these guys, already hard at work! Nice job, Sophia! Those are perfect jumping jacks," and the new students immediately begin with their jumping jacks. At this point, I always give them some positive reinforcement for working hard and brag how they're already doing an awesome job on their first day: "Nice! It's Tyler's first day and he's already doing exactly what he's supposed to do, like a pro!"

These bits of positive reinforcement combined with the social proof of the other students hard at work is a perfect way to help build the expectation of structure and hard work in your classes. The same thing goes for when you're leading stretches - call out the kids who are doing exactly what they're supposed to be and give them plenty of praise in front of the other students. This will encourage the other students to self-monitor and mimic the desired behavior, thus ensuring that all of your students are doing exactly what they should be. If a new student sees 12 other kids focused and working hard, that new student is going to focus and work hard.

Social proof can also be used when considering disciplinary actions. For instance, if a new student is in class and another student is misbehaving, addressing the poor behavior with pushups lets new students and people watching know that you run a tight ship. Having high expectations of students to follow rules ensures they'll get the most out of your classes.

Ultimately, social proof is a way for you to keep your classes organized and maintain student focus. Building good focus in our students not only allows us to accomplish more in our classes since there are fewer distractions, it will help them to build good habits for school and life as they get older and eventually move into professional fields where focus is more than just a preference - it's a necessity for a successful future.

Key Takeaways

- We tend to follow the herd because it's easier than going against it.
- Focus and hard work are necessary habits for children's success.
- Use positive reinforcement combined with social proof to keep classes organized.

PREVENTING LEARNED FEARS

Social proof, while your ally, can also have negative effects, such as learned fears. How we react to things matters, especially to younger children. The younger the child, the more they look to our reactions first to see how they should react to a stimulus. For example, have you ever seen a toddler just learning to walk fall onto their butt? The child doesn't react immediately. Instead, they look to see what their parent's reaction is first. The parent's reaction tells the toddler how they should feel about falling. If the parent gasps and runs over to ask if the toddler is okay, then the child learns that what happened was bad and they shouldn't be okay, so they begin crying because of the parent's worry. This is a never ending cycle. They'll be afraid of falling, which can hold them back for fear of a negative result.

I saw a video the other day that really upset me. It was a child's first birthday party, and the infant sat in their highchair with a cake and a single candle flickering in front of him, smiling and laughing as the guests sang happy birthday. Toward the end of the song, his attention focused on the candle and he reached out to grab the flame, immediately putting out the fire. While I acknowledge a baby's skin is more sensitive than an adult's, it appeared that the baby didn't feel any pain. In that same instant, however, all the guests gasped and yelled and the baby jumped in his seat, immediately starting to wail. It seemed clear to me that the baby wasn't in pain - he was simply scared. The entire room communicated to him with their collective gasp that he should be in pain in a very abrupt manner and it terrified the child to tears. And thus, a fear was born. What a traumatizing experience for a child.

How we react to things teaches children how they should react to things. Young children especially learn through observation, like with the Bobo Doll Experiment. I once had a student, who was fearless. For years she climbed up high and jumped off without reserve. She was awesome. Her father was working on overcoming a terrible fear of heights, and he made some great progress thanks to Exposure Therapy, which we'll discuss a little later. Once the family decided to start group sessions, the daughter saw her father break out in cold sweats, going pale as he clinged to whatever he could reach, and the daughter started to mimic her father's fear response. Now she refuses to climb things that were once so easy for her. When she gets on top of something tall, she grabs whatever she can. Now, she's afraid. Our students look to us and how we react. They learn from us even when we don't realize we're teaching.

Getting back to the toddler who's fallen to their butt, if a parent ignores it or simply encourages them to get up, the child will learn that falling is okay. You just get back up and try again. This is an important lesson to teach children from a young age, because this directly relates to failure and the fear of failure, which has possibly the greatest impact on success. Falling may hurt, but there are levels of injury. A small bump when a toddler falls on their butt isn't a big deal and it shouldn't be made worse than it is. Rather, if a child falls and looks at you for your reaction, remain calm, smile, maybe even chuckle a little as if it's a silly slip-up, and say something like, "Nice fall, buddy. All right, right back up! Let's try again."

Reacting in this much more positive way will teach the child that failure is okay. If you fail once trying to accomplish something, it's not a big deal. You learn from it and try again. If you fail a thousand times trying to accomplish something, it's not a big deal. You learn from those thousand failures and you try again. Though the number varies based on the reference, Thomas Edison famously said, "I have not failed. I've just found 10,000 ways that won't work."

Imagine if Thomas Edison had been taught as a child that failing once meant he shouldn't try again. Imagine if Steve Jobs had been taught that, or Bill Gates, or Jeff Bezos. We wouldn't have smartphones, or the internet, or Amazon! Do you think that any famously successful person hasn't failed a thousand times more than they've succeeded? Failure is the road to success. Countless successful people have said this. Would you ignore a well-watered and well-nourished man in a desert when he tells you that water is just over the next dune to the right? Would you continue straight, ignoring the man who clearly has the information to help you be well-watered and well-nourished as he himself is?

To reiterate my final point on this subject, we must keep our emotions and our fears in check. We should teach caution to our students, but never fear. Caution is the calculated understanding of what could go wrong so we can have a plan in case it does. You'd be amazed how much the smallest comment you make can affect the rest of a child's life. Always teach caution and preparedness, but never teach fear or turning away from a challenge.

The start of this is a child falling or bumping themselves on something, getting some kind of injury. If you overreact, the child will overreact, and you'll teach them to overreact every time something similar happens. Instead, teach them that we all fall and encourage them to get back up to do it again.

FAMOUS FAILURE FOR SUCCESS QUOTES

"There are no secrets to success. It is the result of preparation, hard work, and learning from failure."

-Colin Powell, Retired Four-Star General in the U.S. Army

"A little more persistence, a little more effort, and what seemed hopeless failure may turn to glorious success."
-Elbert Hubbard, Writer, Publisher, Artist, and Philosopher

"Remember your dreams and fight for them. You must know what you want from life. There is just one thing that makes your dream become impossible: the fear of failure."
-Paulo Coelho, Brazilian Lyricist and Novelist

"Failure is simply the opportunity to begin again, this time more intelligently."
-Henry Ford, Founder of Ford Motor Company

"Failures, repeated failures, are finger posts on the road to achievement. One fails forward to success."
-C.S. Lewis, British Writer and Theologian

"The greatest glory in living lies not in never falling, but in rising every time we fall."
-Ralph Waldo Emerson, Lecturer, Philosopher, and Poet

"It is impossible to live without failing at something, unless you live so cautiously that you might as well not have lived at all, in which case you have failed by default."
-J.K. Rowling, British Author, Film Producer, Screenwriter

Just last night, in fact, I had a 6-year-old boy, easily one of the strongest kids in my Mini Ninja classes, do a side vault, jumping with both hands on an object and bringing both legs to one side. He didn't quite jump high enough and whacked his shin on the edge of a wooden box. I've wacked my shins a few hundred times in my years of doing parkour, and it's not great. I walked him through dealing with the pain, first walking over calmly and saying, "Oh, man, I've done that so many times! It doesn't feel good, huh? That's okay, though. Stand up and stomp your foot a bit. Nice job. Now hop up and down a few times. Nice job, man! All right, do you want to sit down for a second with some ice or do you want to jump right back into class?" He asked for ice, but by the time I got back thirty seconds later, he was already back in line and ready to go again.

Notice the process here. He got hurt and I didn't run over. I remained calm, walking over, and casually telling him how many times I've made that same mistake, communicating through my movements and my demeanor that it wasn't a severe injury. Sometimes kids cry because they don't know what to expect. Is the pain going to stay forever? How serious is it? Young children don't understand the difference between a bump and a real injury yet. Another reason kids cry after a minor injury is from embarrassment, so I made sure he didn't feel alone. I, the instructor, the one whom he looks up to because I can do all the stuff he wants to do, have made the same mistake that he just made, and I've made it a lot of times. Why should he be embarrassed if "the coolest guy in the room" has done the same thing a hundred times?

From there, I commiserated with him, telling him I remember how it feels, but notice the wording of it. I didn't say, "Man, that really hurts!" Instead, I minimized and said, "It doesn't feel good, huh?" Two things here. What I didn't do is tell him how it feels. Instead, I asked, which allows him to analyze the pain himself and decide, while at the same time showing him that I care about how he's feeling and I'm helping him work through it.

The second thing is the language choice, getting back to NLP, which I highly encourage every instructor to research. Side note, I honestly think everybody in the world should learn about NLP because of how much word choice can have staggering effects on every aspect of our lives. If I said it hurt, he would have focused on the sensation of pain. Instead, I said, "feel good," which allowed him to focus on the sensation of feeling good and getting better.

Next, I told him it was okay and gave him a few small tasks to get his mind off the pain. Giving him these stomping and hopping tasks does three things. For one, it creates the placebo effect - by implying that the tasks will reduce pain, they do. Secondly, the increased blood flow from mobilizing will help to reduce pain. Lastly, focusing on the action itself will help to distract him from the pain, while my praise and encouragement release the brain's natural "feel good" chemical, dopamine, which also helps with pain management.

To conclude, I gave him the option of sitting down or jumping back into class. There is a language piece here as well, but most of the work is done with the tone of my voice. When I asked if he wanted to sit down and grab some ice, my voice was lower energy and a little bummed out. This combined with the word "sit," which to a 6-year-old implies boring, makes that the lesser option. The second option was to jump right back into class, where I emphasized the word "jump" and increased the energy in my tone, implying a much more fun experience. This along with the idea of jumping instead of sitting is by far the more appealing option.

Still, the pain hadn't subsided quite enough, so he wanted to sit for a bit, but as he saw the other kids continuing to jump and have fun and cheer each other on, he was back in line and ready to go before I could get back with the ice. The whole thing took less than two minutes for the boy to be right back up and playing again, working toward a goal that he failed at just a moment ago, aiming once more toward success, not letting fear of it happening again stop him.

This kind of thing happens every single day to kids all over the world. The problem is when people don't know how to handle the situation. Instead of soothing the child and encouraging them to get back up, people often coddle the child. I saw an example of this while training at a park, where a child somewhere between 8 and 10 hit his shin on a bench trying to jump onto it. The father ran over and picked up the crying child, rocking him and rubbing his back, then sat down with the child for almost 10 minutes. Then they left.

Now, I applaud that father for showing such affection and consoling his son - good on him for being an awesome and caring father. There are just a few issues with this situation as it played out. One, he taught the child to need somebody else to make him feel better instead of teaching him how to be independent and handle the situation himself if his dad wasn't around. Two, he taught the child that getting hurt gets lots of love and affection. This is one of the reasons kids like to flop themselves all over the ground - I know we've all had to work with those kinds of kids. Three, and the worst part, is that they left right after. The child got hurt and they left, not allowing the child the opportunity to try again, meaning the last experience the boy had when trying something new was failure and pain. Do you think he's going to try that again? When the last experience you have is something undesirable, your natural instinct is to avoid that in the future. And that's another way fears are developed.

Every child is different and there are certainly some personalities that will try again despite the memory of pain and failure, sometimes in spite of it, but that's a very small number of the population. All too many people, when a failure is the last thing they experienced, will develop a mental block, a fear of what might happen because of what happened last time. Don't do this to a child. Help build their confidence and competence by helping them to get past that learned fear by trying again right away instead of walking away from it. Encouraging a child to get back up and try again is the best way to protect them from being trapped in their head with learned fears for the rest of their lives. Encourage children to fight fears before they take hold, using each failure as a learning opportunity for success.

Key Takeaways

- Children mimic. Be careful what fears you express to them.
- Consider carefully how your actions can contribute to the development of long-term fears.
- Encourage children to try again after failure or minor injury to avoid mental blocks. (Obviously not after severe injuries.)

WALKING THROUGH FEARS

This is easily one of the most important things we do as instructors, because fear is the greatest threat to a child's success. If intelligent people were afraid to experiment, if resourceful people were afraid to invest, if they were taught from a young age that fear is a reason to not do something, then we would still be uncivilized primitives rather than the technologically advanced society that we are today. The world's greatest advances came from somebody doing something that scared them. If we want to powerfully impact a child's life and potentially the future of humankind, helping children break fears is the most potent skill we can master.

Maybe you're a teacher with a student afraid to do a presentation, or maybe you're a parent with a child afraid to spend their first night away from home or afraid to try their first dance class. Teaching Ninja Warrior, I often have kids that are afraid to do monkey bars or rings.

Teaching Parkour, I often have kids who are afraid of jumping across a gap with a small drop or a smaller gap with a bigger drop. Teaching Capoeira, I often have kids who are afraid to sing in front of others. Everybody has fears. Every day, I work with at least one child to help them break a fear. And every day I try to face at least one of my own fears, whether it's learning a new flip, trying a new marketing idea, writing a new song that might not be as good as my last favorite that I wrote, and so on.

Every instructor should train ourselves for this, because we can't teach it to others until we practice it ourselves. Zig Ziglar put forth my two favorite acronyms for FEAR as a reminder that we choose how we'll handle it: 1) Forget Everything And Run - forget the lessons and experiences you've had, ignore the proof that people like Bill Gates, Simone Biles, Oprah, and countless other successes have served as, and turn away from the challenge; or 2) Face Everything And Rise - face the things that scare you head-on, look a challenge in the eye and don't ask the question "Is it possible?" Instead, ask the question, "HOW is it possible?" Find the answer and reap the benefits of your success.

Confidence-Building Affirmations

- It's okay to be afraid. It's not okay to let fear hold you back.
- It's not a matter of whether you can or can't - it's a matter of how you're going to.
- Face Everything And Rise.

Only when we can work through our own fears can we help the next generations to work through their own. We should experience every piece of breaking through fears in order to help others walk through theirs. We should be able to recognize the anxiety that comes with facing something that terrifies us. Work on facing your own fears, and helping students face theirs becomes much easier. And that's when we start affecting the greatest numbers.

There are a few basic steps to breaking any fear, and really it comes down to understanding. In the amazing book, "The 7 Habits of Highly Effective People" by Stephen Covey, Habit 6 is "Seek first to understand, then to be understood." This is important in all our interactions with others, especially when it comes to breaking a fear. To eliminate something from our lives, or at the very least to work past it, we must seek first to understand.

I should preface that the following technique only works with rational fears. For irrational fears or problematic thoughts, I highly recommend Cognitive Behavioral Therapy (CBT) to adapt thoughts and experiences to a more beneficial way of life.

We can use this when working with kids on obstacles or any other rational fears they may have. Of course, the conversation will look slightly different depending who you're helping to work through it. On the next page is an example of when I helped a 6-year-old during a birthday party.

ME:	*Why are you afraid of the rings?*
6YO:	*I'm afraid I'll fall and break my head open.* (Kids can get pretty graphic sometimes. I don't know what they're watching, but sometimes they shock me.)
ME:	*Okay, but I'm here and I wouldn't let you fall, right?*
6YO:	*Yeah.*
ME:	*And we've got this super soft mat under you too, right?*
6YO:	*Yeah.*
ME:	*Do you want to be able to do the rings?*
6YO:	*Yeah, but I'm scared.*
ME:	*It's okay to be scared, bud. I'm here with you right now, though, and I can help you do it so you're not scared. And then you'll get better and better at it and soon you won't need my help at all and you'll be the fastest person on the rings. Would you like to be super brave and keep getting better at things and keep getting stronger?*
6YO:	*Yeah.*
ME:	*Nice! I knew you were brave! Let's do this, buddy. You've got this!*

He fell off the second ring onto the soft mat and realized his fears weren't as realistic as he thought. After that, he practiced non-stop without me spotting him, forgetting about all his friends that were running around and playing as he kept working. That day he learned that sometimes things that seem scary at first aren't always that scary, and that falling isn't a bad thing as long as you get back up and try again. He came back a few weeks later, super excited to tell me that he did all the rings at the park and couldn't wait to show me. With the right encouragement, the lesson he learned in that single interaction - pushing past fears, hard work, and dedication - can set a child on a straight path toward success!

Think about something in your life that you're afraid to do, whether it's going skydiving, taking martial arts classes, learning to dance, or whatever. Run yourself through the questions above for breaking rational fears. I've never felt more empowered, like I could do anything, than when I push past a fear. When you make a decision to push past your fears and do something that scares you, the world opens itself up to you. It's proof that you're capable of more than you think you are. Sometimes doing a thing is scary, but not as scary as not doing it.

If I hadn't learned this lesson at a young age, I wouldn't have opened AMP Academy, and I wouldn't have been able to help all the kids I've helped learn that same lesson over the years. The most important thing we can do for any child is to help them push past their fears. Success is on the other side of fear and failure.

Key Takeaways

- Be patient. Every child's needs are different.
- Be observant. Every child's needs are different.
- Be kind. Every child's needs are different.

USING EXPOSURE THERAPY

There are two types of fears: Rational and Irrational. We discussed rational fears above, the kind that we can explain and work through using logic by teaching students the right questions to ask to get past them. In this chapter, we'll discuss irrational fears - phobias - the kind that are so deeply embedded in a person that it defines the way they live their lives. These are much stronger and more challenging to work with because they can't be worked through using logic, and are thus a greater risk for holding students back from success.

Don't dismay, though - there's a way to help break these kinds of fears too. Many psychologists argue that Exposure Therapy is the most effective treatment for phobias and anxieties. It was developed to help people overcome their fears, and allows people to confront them in small doses rather than avoiding their fears altogether, thus reinforcing and legitimizing their fears, making them harder to overcome over time. Exposure therapy, then, helps those who use it to stop avoiding what scares them. Sure, avoidance might feel good at the time, but it always makes something come on stronger later. We can only run so far before things catch up with us.

In an effort to reduce the sensation of fear and eliminate the urge to avoid situations where their fear might be present, exposure therapy allows a subject to experience that fear in a safe and controlled environment. It helps people to live happier lives by not letting fear control them and hold them back.

There are different levels of exposure therapy and each level will be appropriate for different situations. For instance, it's not a great idea to have somebody with an intense fear of heights stand atop the Empire State Building, a quarter-mile in the sky with powerful winds whipping past them. In some cases, it may be best to start a little smaller, only asking them to imagine the feared situation in their mind's eye.

Let's take a quick look at the different varieties of exposure therapy and discuss what situations for which each would be most ideal:

1. **Imaginal Exposure** - Using one's imagination. This type of exposure is when a person imagines the feared situation and places themselves in that situation in their mind. This is the least extreme form and is only necessary for the most intense fear response, though it can be skipped in most cases.

2. **Graded Exposure** - Slowly expose somebody to their fear at a more intense level, bit by bit. For instance, having somebody

with a fear of heights climbing a ladder, where they take only one step at a time and allow their fear response to dissipate before taking the next step.

3. **In Vivo Exposure** - Full exposure. This one is by far the most intense and ideally the final step in the order of operations. In this form of exposure therapy, a person with a fear of spiders might be handed a tarantula and directed to handle it for a certain amount of time.

How we handle these fear responses with children is vital for their future success. A child should never be forced into an exposure therapy situation, as that can cause emotional harm and I would argue that it's abusive. Children, instead, can and should be reasoned with to help them break these fears. This means that you need permission from them.

Using the fear of heights as an example, since this is most common when helping children in my particular field, the order of questions to get a child's permission to help them overcome their fear should be this:

1. Is it scary being up this high?
2. Do you like being afraid of that?
3. Would you like me to help you to not be afraid of it?
4. Is it okay if I hold your hand while you walk closer to the edge?
5. Is it okay if I let go of your hand? I'll still be right here.
6. Okay, are you ready? Go ahead, bud Remember, I'm right here.

The next step is to never abandon them while they're trusting you.

Be a constant support so they know you're right there and you have them just in case they fall, but don't overhelp them, or you'll actually teach them that they can't do it without your help. As they work toward their goal, combatting their fear, reiterate words of encouragement and remind them that they're doing it by themselves. You being there to support them isn't the same as you doing it for them. Help them build confidence by praising them for the hard work they're doing and tell them how proud of them you are for being so brave.

Alway, always, *always* praise a child who's just confronted their fears. We want children to understand that facing fears is rewarded. This is how we can ensure that children face their fears in adulthood, not letting fears hold them back from success. Remember that growth can *only* occur outside of our comfort zones. If we're always comfortable, we'll always remain the same. There's no reason to change or grow if everything is easy and convenient and comfortable. We only learn, we only grow, when our current reality isn't sufficient for success. For your own success, try to be uncomfortable every day, and you'll always rise to the level of comfort in that situation.

Key Takeaways

- Always encourage students and be supportive as they face fears.
- Be patient and sympathetic as students build their confidence to try something scary.
- Growth can only occur outside one's comfort zone.

SPOTTING & SUPPORTING

I talk a lot about these physical experiences, like monkey bars and jumping, primarily because children are most strongly influenced by tangible things. Their psyches are affected by their physical experiences. Building confidence in their bodies builds confidence in their minds. Pushing their bodies in their youth will teach them healthy habits for pushing their minds in the future. If you want a child to be successful, they need to go through these experiences of being uncomfortable and working through it, being given responsibility and rising to the challenge, failing and still getting up to try again. It's easiest to teach through physical experiences and they will have the greatest impact on a young child's developing mindset.

Spotting and support are two sides of the same coin, and every instructor should know the right way to do both. Spotting refers to physical support through external challenges, while support refers to emotional spotting through internal challenges, and the principles remain the same for both. There are different scenarios in which spotting or support might be required, like when teaching a student the monkey bars versus how to do a backflip, or when a child is suffering due to shyness versus bullying. Each situation is going to call for a different type of spotting or support to get students through the challenge and come out stronger on the other side. So how do you know which is best for what?

Well, there's a fine line between helping and doing all or most of the work. In a situation where you're teaching a backflip, where the child's physical safety is at greater risk, you want to take most of the responsibility for the child completing the movement. You're obviously not going to just say, "Well, good luck!" You're teaching a child to go upside-down, flipping over their head - kind of an important part of the body - something they've certainly never done before and something that can have severe consequences if they do it incorrectly.

LEVELS OF SPOTTING		
Level 1	Heavy Support	The instructor takes most of the child's weight and performs most of the movement for the child.
Level 2	Moderate Support	The instructor takes a part of the child's weight and allows the child to perform most of the movement on their own, helping to ensure the most important part of the movement and the child's safety.
Level 3	Light Support	The instructor allows the child to work through the movement themselves, but is still present and prepared to ensure the child's safety.
Level 4	Moral Support	The instructor is present but takes none of the child's weight, allowing the child to do the entirety of the movement themselves.

For higher risk maneuvers, like flips, I obviously recommend Level 1 spotting to start. I've seen a lot of parents and even some instructors use Level 1 spotting for things like monkey bars or cargo nets, which can be extremely harmful to a students' psychological development. For something like that, I recommend Level 3, or Level 2 spotting at most if a child is very scared, but I would never recommend Level 1 spotting for anything relatively low risk that allows children to face a fear or challenge. If it doesn't require a physical skill the child doesn't have, Level 1 spotting isn't necessary.

It's important for us to understand what we communicate through our actions as we help children, even if we don't say something flat out. When we use Level 1 spotting on something like monkey bars, it tells the child that they can't do it on their own. This can result in a condition called Learned Helplessness, and it can negatively affect a person for their entire lives.

American psychologist Martin Seligman began researching Learned Helplessness in 1967 using a controversial and upsetting experiment involving dogs and shock collars. *WARNING: This is an upsetting experiment for its cruelty toward animals, so if you'd like to skip over the details of the experiment, please skip the following two paragraphs.*

In this experiment, Seligman had three groups of dogs. Group 1 was a control group that was simply put in a harness for some time and were then released - nothing significant was observed during this part of the experiment. Groups 2 and 3 were paired with shock collars. In the experiment, the dogs in Group 2 could stop the shock for both groups by pressing a lever, while the dogs in Group 3 could do nothing to stop the shock. Essentially, no matter what the dogs in Group 3 did, the shock seemed to stop at random.

In the second portion of the experiment, the same groups of dogs were placed in a "shuttle box" - a large box divided into two halves by a low partition. On one half of the shuttle box, the floor was electrified to administer shocks by researchers, while the other side could not shock the study's participants. The ultimate results of the study were that the dogs in Groups 1 and 2 quickly found their way onto the other side of the shuttle box, thus protecting themselves from the shock on the other side. However, many of the dogs from Group 3, who previously had no way of stopping the administered shocks, merely laid down and whined as the shock continued, waiting for it to stop on its own, not bothering to even try to escape.

That is both sickening and heartbreaking to me as a dog lover, and it's exactly what happens to a child who is carried through life without the chance to be their own person and make their own mistakes.

If instructors don't push students to do their part, students will learn that nothing they do will have an effect. If their work ethic played no part in success when they were younger, there's no reason to work hard as they get older either - they'll get to the end anyway, through no effort of their own, and they'll be praised for having accomplished something that they put no effort into. Why should they work? Why put in any effort when somebody else can do it for them and they can reap the reward? Why try to get out of a bad situation on their own when somebody else will just save them?

Be very careful not to allow your spotting to become relied upon in safer situations. Instead, teach students how to learn and accomplish things on their own so they can become self-sufficient. Remember that independence is the door to success and responsibility is the key. Allow students to be responsible for their own outcomes and they'll be stronger for it. Children should learn that they can do things on their own. They should learn that success isn't handed to them - it's earned. One of the most important lessons my father taught me when I was growing up was, "I'm not always going to be around. One day, you'll need to do something, and I won't be there to hold your hand. You need to learn how to do it on your own." When students learn that their actions determine an outcome, they'll make better choices.

Seligman tried demonstrations, rewards, and even threats to cure the Group 3 dogs of their Learned Helplessness, but none worked. The only cure for it was to physically put the dogs through the motions of doing it on their own with some Level 1 spotting. It took repeating this at least twice before the dogs realized they had control over their own fate and started jumping over the barrier on their own.

It's much harder to cure this condition than it is to simply prevent it altogether, so be sure to use the appropriate level of spotting in every situation and only praise for what the student actually did. When children are doing a challenging obstacle, let them do most of it. That's not to say not to help at all, but a child's actions have consequences, and they should know that. If they don't put in the effort on an obstacle, they won't succeed at that obstacle. If they put in all their effort, you should only need to provide Level 3 spotting or at most Level 2. This will teach them to work hard and that they control their own success. This is one of the greatest ways we can help develop a child's strength, confidence, and work ethic.

In a similar vein, although perhaps slightly off, I'd like to relate a quick story that is a perfect example of what to *never do*. I had a new student in a class of 4-to-6-year-olds and we were working on the cargo net that day - something like a fishing net, but with bigger openings. It was the first time many of the students had worked on that obstacle. As I was spotting another student, I gave the new student the greenlight to begin. He was nervous to put weight on the leg that he put on the cargo net because it kept moving, so I gave him some quick advice, telling him to reach high and stand up, planning to help him more directly once I finished spotting the first child.

I couldn't believe what happened next. As the first student finished and I was walking back to help the new student, I heard his mother say from the side, "You don't have to do it if it's too hard, sweetie," and I nearly tripped over myself. This mother had just told her child that if something was too hard he could just give up. She'd just told him that she didn't think he could do it and there was no point in even trying. That's what I heard, and I know that's what the child heard subconsciously too. This was Permissive Parenting at its most blatant. The boy let go of the cargo net and started to walk to the back of the line, but I stopped him and called him back over.

Obviously, I couldn't show how upset the mother's comment had made me, but I could at least teach the child that he *could* do it, even if his mom didn't think he could. And I hoped his mother might learn a better way to teach than just telling him to give up. I got down on my knee and did some Level 2 spotting, telling him to put his hands high up and moving his hands a little higher when he didn't reach quite high enough. Then I had him put his foot on the cargo net and told him it was going to swing out, but not to worry about it, just hold on and stand up.

After a little one-on-on and some Level 3 spotting as he got more comfortable, the new student was able to take three steps across the cargo net before dropping on his first turn. He made it more than halfway by the end of the class and he was so excited that he did it completely on his own! I was able to teach him the most important lesson, that he could do it and giving up wasn't the answer. I can only hope that my single interaction with him is enough to combat the negative support his mother had provided for him on that day.

Sometimes we'll only have one day with a student and we want to teach them everything we can to help them become successful adults. Always encourage students to try their hardest at everything they do and to never give up. Encourage them to do things on their own, as long as safety isn't a huge risk, and teach them to gauge risk if there is. We want every child to know they can accomplish anything with a bit of hard work and dedication. Only by building the habit of trying and trying until they finally succeed can we truly give them the roadmap to success.

Key Takeaways

- Level 1 Spotting should only be used when there is high risk.
- Praise kids for what they actually accomplished, not what you helped them with, but their own contribution to their success.
- Allow kids to build their confidence by helping them minimally, not doing it for them.

ENSURING EQUALITY OVER FAVORITISM

It's vital that we treat every student the same. That's not groundbreaking information, yet no matter how aware we are, we will still fall short in this category because we're human and being conscious of this goes against human nature. However, we want to do our absolute best to recognize when we're giving any kind of preferential treatment to students, regardless of to what extent, in what way, and why.

Third-grade teacher and anti-racism activist Jane Elliot performed a very famous experiment in 1968 known as the Blue Eyes vs. Brown Eyes experiment. In an effort to explain to her third-grade class about Martin Luther King Jr's assassination by teaching them about descrimination, she separated the students by blue eyes and brown eyes and explained that there was a chemical in our bodies called melanin that caused intelligence. The darker a person's eyes, the smarter they are, she explained, and since people with brown eyes had more melanin, it meant that they were smarter than people with blue eyes. "People with blue eyes," she said, "sit around and do nothing. You give them something nice and they wreck it."

Elliot then went on to explain the rules of the day. Kids with blue eyes had to use disposable cups when they drank from the water fountain. Kids with brown eyes could say whatever they wanted to the kids with blue eyes and they wouldn't get in trouble. The brown-eyed kids became cruel, and the blue-eyed kids began to feel the effects of the experiment very quickly. Blue-eyed students were making more mistakes that usual and brown-eyed students that had once been shy and reserved began to take on leadership roles with their new-found confidence in their intelligence and superiority over blue-eyed kids, demonstrating once again that our students will become how we treat them. It's horrifying to imagine and hard to believe, yet you can see it for yourself in the documentary called "A Class Divided," which takes one iteration of her experiment and allows us to follow it in all it's repugnance.

The following Monday, the roles were reversed, and brown-eyed kids were told how dumb and lazy they were. The blue-eyed kids were less cruel to the brown-eyed kids, however, presumably because they'd been on the other side of it and they may have not wanted to make others feel the torture they'd gone through only a few days earlier.

This experiment was performed to explain descrimination to children under ten years old, but it teaches a valuable lesson to us as instructors too. Obviously, we should never treat students poorly for any reason, especially because of their skin color, socio-economic status, or really anything that differentiates them from other students just out of basic human decency. Treating all students equally is much easier than treating all students fairly.

For example, when we think about this in the context of operant conditioning, we want to make sure all kids are praised or disciplined fairly. If we have a student that gets in a lot of trouble in classes, never focuses, and always earns push-ups, it's easy to give them the push-ups they earned when breaking a rule. It's more difficult to give those same push-ups to another student who is always focused and always works hard despite them having broken the same rule, yet it's important to do that so you're not giving preferential treatment. Consistency is key.

Dutch primatologist Frans de Waal and Sarah Brosnan, who studied cooperation and reciprocity in the early 2000's, also performed a study on the effects of unequal pay. In this study, five capuchin monkeys were paired with experimenters. Two of the five monkeys received the same reward (a cucumber) for completing a task, one received a greater reward (a grape) for completing the same task, one received the greater reward (grape) without completing a task, and the last received a grape without the presence of a partner.

When the monkeys were paired with a partner that received the same reward for completing the same task, there were no problems. However, once the monkeys saw their partner receiving a greater reward for completing the same task, the monkey started to reject the cucumber, the lesser reward. In the instance where a monkey received the greater reward of a grape while performing no task, the intensity of refusal increased from merely not taking the cucumber, to instead taking the cucumber and throwing it back at the experimenter who'd given it to them.

It's a primal reaction. When one person receives a reward for doing the same thing another is doing with no reward or with a lesser reward, the desired behavior is abandoned. If you have a class of ten kids and nine of them are behaving while one isn't, discipline may be required, but first consider why that's happening. Think about whether you've been fair in your praise and disciplinary actions. Are any children receiving preferential treatment? Are any children receiving a greater reward for performing the same task?

When a student misbehaves, we should consider whether we've done something to lead to this. If the answer is no, perfect! Move on and begin the process of training that person to behave better. If the answer is yes, then it's time to figure out how you can level the playing field for them and doing so should help to modify that student's behavior for the better.

Lastly, due to the importance of equal treatment from instructors in the development of children, I'd like to talk very briefly about two Cognitive Biases as we flow into the idea of favoritism. These Cognitive Biases are known as the Halo Effect and the Horn Effect.

The Halo Effect is the bias that occurs when somebody performs well in one area of their life, so people assume they'll perform well in all areas of their life. For instance, if somebody does well in their job, it isn't evidence they're also a good husband or father. A student coming from an upper-middle class home doesn't mean that student is more intelligent or better behaved than other students. More often it occurs based on looks, however. Just because somebody is attractive doesn't mean that they're a hard worker or a good person or intelligent, etc.

The Horn Effect is the inverse, the bias that assumes somebody who performs poorly in one area of their life must perform poorly in all areas of their life. For instance, just because somebody is unattractive in a photo because they're unshaven or wearing holey jeans doesn't mean that they're a bad person, or lazy, or behave poorly. Just because somebody isn't as well-off financially doesn't mean that they aren't a hard worker or aren't intelligent, yet the Horn Effect is the phenomenon that makes us believe that subconsciously.

Again, while these effects often occur because of looks, they don't have to be tied to that. A family's financial status, the way they dress, or even if they have a historic name (like the Vanderbilts or Kennedys) can all affect the way we perceive that student. As instructors, we must recognize these cognitive biases in ourselves and actively work to ensure that all of our students are treated fairly independent of socio-economic backgrounds, historical family name, appearance, clothing, or anything other than the merits of their performance. The first step to curbing the Halo and Horn Effects is awareness of when it's affecting us so we can modify our own behavior also. This will allow us to educate children to have better attitudes, greater focus, better grades, be more productive, and ultimately become more successful in adulthood.

As we move into the topic of favoritism, let's first define it. Favoritism is "the practice of giving unfair preferential treatment to one person or group at the expense of another." So, avoiding favoritism doesn't mean we can't have favorites. We shouldn't have favorites, mind you. That's just really hard because we're human and human nature causes us to prefer people like ourselves. We want to be conscious of how we're treating our students and making sure we're giving every student a fair opportunity for success.

Awareness is the first step to change, so what traits inevitably make students make students favorites? The students we tend to favor usually work hardest in class, or are most successful in class, thus perpetuating the Halo Effect once more. A child's positivity also comes into play when favorites emerge, but there's another factor that sets some students apart, and that's their focus, which ultimately occurs due to something known as Delayed Gratification.

Psychologist and Professor Walter Mischel studied Delayed Gratification at Stanford University in 1972 with the Stanford Marshmallow Experiment. This experiment essentially gave children a choice to either receive a small reward immediately, or wait a few minutes to receive double the reward. The rewards themselves were marshmallows, hence the name, or pretzel sticks, based on the child's preference.

When the subjects of the study were interviewed years later, the ones that delayed gratification for the double reward were found to have had better life outcomes in terms of health (such as BMI goals), grades in school, and a variety of other standard measures of success. Knowing this, we want to help students build willpower, a key attribute of delayed gratification.

The experiment has been replicated many times over the years and, much to my surprise, found that children have a better grasp on delayed gratification now than back then, which is great news for the instructors of today. In the original experiment, just over 30% delayed gratification for the full 10 minutes and received the double reward. In a late 80's New York City replica of the experiment, 38% showed delayed gratification, and 60% of the children delayed gratification for the double reward in a 2002-to-2012 replication.

If we can assure a reward that children value, then their focus is more assured. We are more likely than our predecessors to have structured classes, as long as we use this information appropriately, and thus contribute to the future success of all our students.

But I digress. Delayed gratification is just another reason why we might find ourselves favoring certain students. Now, let's return to the importance of not falling into favoritism.

When all students are treated equally, they have equal opportunity for success. When we treat some students favorably and others less so, it doesn't afford the less favored students the same opportunities in class, which means they don't have the same opportunities for success in life. Every child deserves equal attention and thus equal opportunity for success.

One trick to achieve this is to always spread out your positive feedback. For instance, when I have a class of Mini Ninjas, ages 4-6, I use a combination of positive reinforcement and self-monitoring to get other students to mirror the positive action. When most of the class is stretching appropriately, but one child keeps falling over on purpose (Tommy, for the sake of this example), I walk around the group of stretching kids and say with a positive and upbeat tone, "Look at that! Ryan's got perfect form, staying on his feet. Who else has perfect form today? Let's see. It looks like Charlotte has some pretty good form. Carly is doing great! Look how straight that leg is! Nice! And Tommy is back on his feet with super straight legs! I don't know, Tommy might actually have better form than Ryan right now! Awesome work, buddy!"

In that example, which is the favorite? I'm clearly using Ryan as an example of how I want the others to act, but I'm spreading the praise amongst all the students, bouncing around the circle so each student gets attention for their hard work. While Tommy was falling over and rolling around on the floor only moments ago, he heard everybody else getting praise for doing what they were supposed to and he self-monitored so he would get praise himself. Once he adjusted to do what I wanted him to do, I immediately praised how great he was doing.

We like positive attention in the same way that any pet does. If you yell at a dog for tearing up your couch, they slump away and hide, but when you crouch down, excited to see them, petting them and praising them, they rub into you and prance, sniffing and licking you, unable to contain themselves with all the attention. We as people are the same way, and children are people. When we receive positive attention, we thrive on it. We revel in it. We do our best to receive positive attention from those we care about, and children do the same.

If you spread your positive attention around the room to all your students, all of the students will build the habit of working harder regularly to get that same positive attention in the future. This will lead to a more organized class and more self-aware and respectful students. These are the kinds of habits all children should have to be successful.

On the other side of things, when you have a clear favorite and you only give them attention, your students will start to act out, because any attention from you is better than no attention from you. If you discipline them for doing something wrong, they're still getting attention from you. You're still recognizing them, and it's easier to rebel than it is to work hard. Be fair to your students and you'll have a much more pleasant group of hardworking students to guide on their path to success.

Key Takeaways

- Spread out your praise equally amongst your students.
- Be aware of the Halo and Horn Effects. Awareness is the first step to change.
- Be consistent and fair. All crimes stand alone - who commits them is irrelevant.

LEARNING STYLES

Have you ever noticed that you learn differently from others? Some people prefer to read a manual or look at pictures to learn something. Others prefer listening to lectures, while some would rather just jump right in and figure it out on their own. As instructors, it's important for us to remember that not everybody is like us. What works for you might not work for somebody else. To teach most effectively, we want to understand what the different learning styles are, how to identify a person's preference for one style over another, and lastly how to communicate best with different learners.

Let's first start out by identifying what the primary different types of learning are.

- Visual - Learn by seeing/sight
- Auditory - Learn by hearing/sound
- Kinesthetic - Learn by doing/experience

We prefer to teach the same way we prefer to learn, but as we established earlier, everybody is different. There are people who love audiobooks because they can consume them faster and retain more information, while some can't focus when somebody is talking and they need the tactile sensation of a book in their hands in order to retain information. Others hold information more easily if it appears visually by watching videos.

Given this, instructors want to incorporate multiple styles of teaching into our everyday lives, which can be challenging. While we can see the value of doing things a certain way, we may also think it a waste of time to describe something three ways when, in our minds, one is enough. Still, if we want all of our students to excel, it's time to open ourselves to the idea of outputting information differently than we prefer to intake the information.

Visual Learners

Visual Learners like to watch demonstrations. These generally appear to be paying more attention since they watch your every movement while you're talking or demonstrating, so it's important to be expressive and communicate as much as you can with your movements. In class, somebody may ask to see something a few times before they're ready to try it on their own. These learners typically prefer to be closer to the demonstration. They like seeing the details of a movement or concept. When demonstrating to these types of learners, it's useful to exaggerate movements so each detail is clearly visible, making it easier for them to replicate when it's their turn. Having a curriculum that students can visually see is also a huge benefit for visual learners.

Auditory Learners

Auditory learners like to listen to explanations. Even when reading, they typically play a voice in their head so they can hear it being said. In class you might see these students looking anywhere but at you, and when you try to call them out for not paying attention, they can fire back what you just said almost verbatim. Auditory learners ask a lot of questions. They like to confirm what you said by repeating or rephrasing it to make sure they heard right. They love when you ask questions and they get to repeat back what you just said in their own words. It's beneficial to use variety in vocal tones to help auditory learners retain information. Using accents, sound effects, alliteration, and rhyming are great ways to keep these learners engaged and help them get the most out of their time with you.

Kinesthetic Learners

Kinesthetic learners like to learn by doing. These are the students who love to demonstrate or who always ask if they can try it. They often have a hard time sitting or standing still when you're teaching - instead you'll find them hanging on things, spinning around, or bouncing. It can be distracting for us as instructors, but it's important to remember that some children need this movement to help them retain information. For kinesthetic learners, it's usually helpful to have them do something rather than have them *not* do something. For instance, "stand still and listen" isn't as effective for them as "pick up one leg and listen." Having them position their bodies a certain way while you're talking, or allowing one to demonstrate after you've finished explaining can be a great way to help them learn.

Learning Combinations

As you read the different styles of learning, you probably noticed that you fall into a few categories. That's because learning is a spectrum. We have the capacity to learn in all three ways, and the topic can actually affect our learning preference also. Think about it like a sliding scale. Imagine that you have 10 skill points to divide amongst three categories: Visual, Auditory, and Kinesthetic. When you divide up those skill points into the various categories, there will always be one category that's filled higher than the others. For instance, I am more of a visual learner with a high auditory preference also, so my skill point breakdown looks like this: Visual - 4 points; Auditory - 4 points; Kinesthetic - 2 points.

No one style of learning is better than another. A student's capacity to learn is greatly influenced by the teaching style of their instructors. As instructors ourselves, we must recognize that we hold the key to a child's learning. They are responsible for paying attention and trying to take in the information, and we are responsible for conveying the information in a way that is most effective for them to understand it. Get comfortable with the different kinds of learning styles and recognize that for each learning style, there's a respective teaching style that works best with it. If you have a student who is struggling, try using a different teaching style and watch how much better they perform.

Identifying Learning Styles by Language Patterns

Language cues can also help us identify a student's learning preference. You'll hear a lot about this should you decide to research Neurolinguistic Programming, and these cues are used a lot by salespeople to build rapport with customers, making it more likely that a person will buy from them. For our purposes, though, they're extremely valuable in helping students learn.

For example, visual learners are more likely to use visual language when they speak, using phrases like, "I *see* what you mean," "I can *see* that you're upset," or "That *looks* good to me!" A visual learner struggling with something might say, "I don't *see* the point." With these types of learners, it's useful to use their preferred word choice. "Can you *imagine* being the fastest person in the class?" or "*See*, I told you you could do it!"

This happens completely naturally and unintentionally. In fact, you'll start to see this now even as you read this book. In fact, I did it in the previous sentence when I said, "You'll start to *see* this." If I'd been heavier on the Auditory side of things, I might have said something like, "You'll *hear* me use auditory cues throughout the book." The language I use is heavily visual and auditory, which is perfect since visual and auditory learners are the greatest majority of the adult population.

Numbers will vary based on where you look, but Visual Learners are about 60% of the adult population, while 30% of adults are Auditory Learners and 10% of adults are Kinesthetic. Fascinatingly, these numbers are significantly different in the child population, with only 29% being Visual Learners, 34% Auditory, and a staggering 37% Kinesthetic, with about 30% of those actually being mixed learning styles. With children, the gross majority learn better through Kinesthetic means with Visual or Auditory as secondary preferences for learning.

An auditory learner will use language more like, "I *hear* what you're saying," and "*Sounds* good to me!" For these learners, it's best if you can vary your speech patterns. Low and slow sometimes, high and fast at others, maybe high and slow or low and fast when appropriate. Use impressions and accents to keep an auditory learner's attention.

Kinesthetic learners use language like, "It just doesn't *feel* right," or "I don't *get* it." For these types of learners, it's helpful to have them do something while you're talking. Try having them mimic the hand position for a specific obstacle. Have them mirror you as you get into funky positions to draw their attention. Teaching kinesthetic learners can sometimes be frustrating because it's difficult to tell when they're paying attention. That's the major challenge - identifying when a kinesthetic learner is actually learning or is just distracted. Be patient.

With kids 7 and under, I recommend using all the techniques at once. Big, expressive movements with your bodies to help keep kids looking at you instead of around the room; varying vocal tones, accents, different voices or impressions, alliteration, rhyming, and other auditorily pleasing techniques; and using different body positions, a command for a single bounce, huge motions to put hands by their sides, or counting fingers with you as you give them three things to remember. Use all these techniques in older classes also, but you can be more subtle. With younger kids, you want to be just a little over the top.

Remember Habit 5 from The 7 Habits of Highly Successful People: "Seek first to understand, then to be understood." Identify learning preferences by a student's language use, then use that language to communicate with them. Incorporate all three learning styles into your teaching style and you'll find that your students will be more engaged and work harder in class. They'll learn better and retain information easier when you can adjust your explanations for the people who need to see, hear, or feel it differently. The better you can modify your teaching styles to match your students' learning styles, the better chance they'll have for success.

Key Takeaways

- Your students' learning styles might not match your teaching style.
- Identify learning styles by observing a student's behavior and the words they use when talking.
- Incorporate techniques for all learning styles into your teaching style for maximum benefit to all students.

SETTING GOALS

Goals are more than a recommendation for success - they're a requirement, because if you don't know where you're going, you'll never get there. Before we go any further, I'd like to make a clear distinction between goals and dreams. A dream is something that you want to happen, something you'd love to happen, something you wish would happen. A goal is something you're consciously working toward and is going to happen. Dreams can only be desired. Goals can be attained.

Rarely do good things just fall into somebody's lap without them working for it. I know a few very successful people, and some of my other friends always say, "They're so lucky!" But I believe we make our own luck by opening ourselves to opportunity. By setting goals, we know where we want to go, so when an opportunity comes by that helps us get there, it seems lucky. If we didn't know where we wanted to go, though, then that opportunity could well be ignored.

As a brief aside, there's a fantastically intelligent British magician/mentalist/performer named Derren Brown who's produced a number of fascinating experiments that can be found on YouTube, and I highly recommend them all if you're interested in understanding the human psyche better. The one I'll direct you to when it comes to the idea of luck is "The Secret of Luck," which aired in 2011. It dives into the world of a pessimist who considered himself unlucky, but it turned out that he was just blind to the opportunity that presented itself to him every day. This episode will absolutely change the way you understand luck. Back to goals.

Encouraging students to set goals will give them greater opportunity for success. Having dreams is good for helping you establish goals, but having goals can ensure that you'll someday attain what you've set out for. Business consultant George T. Doran developed a few guidelines for setting goals to increase the likelihood of achieving them and released them in a paper in 1981. They've been modified a number of times by various people, but the heart of these guidelines remains the same. Develop SMART Goals for increased success.

SMART Goals

- Specific (Simple, Sensible, Significant)
- Measurable (Meaningful, Motivating)
- Achievable (Agreed, Attainable)
- Relevant (Realistic and Resourced, Results-based)
- Time-bound (Time-based, Time-limited, Time-sensitive)

Each variation is valuable in its own way. Some relate more to business, while some target the average person, but all have the same idea behind them. Setting goals like, "Someday I'll be a football player," or, "Someday I'll have a million dollars," or "Someday I'll land a backflip" doesn't work, because "someday" breaks the T rule of SMART.

Something like, "I want to be able to make it across the rings and back without falling by June," is highly Specific, Measurable because it's quantitative (if there are 6 rings, there and back makes 12, so you can gauge when you hit 4, 6, 8, etc.), Achievable because there's plenty of time to work up to it, Relevant because it relates to their overall goal for grip strength, and Time-bound because they've set a deadline. Is it possible to achieve that goal without saying it aloud? Yes, but like I said at the beginning of the book, saying something aloud gives it sticking power. By saying it out loud to the class and instructor, now it's possible for us to help them achieve it. We can hold them accountable. We can give them advice and workout routines to help them. We can support them because they've given us something so tangible.

This book is something I've wanted to write for years, and I've been working on what concepts would be in it for a long time. I put so much planning into it, but I never took the steps to actually finish it. It took flying across the country to a business seminar, telling somebody about this dream of mine, and them asking when it would be done for me to realize I didn't have an answer. So I decided on one. I made a public post that very day telling the world I would publish this book in April 2020. That self-imposed deadline has pushed me to spend 8 hours a day writing while continuing to teach and manage my business through a pandemic-imposed closure. It's the first week of April and I'm 38 pages away from finishing my final revision, which includes the addition of this story to prove that accountability works. Check out the publish date. Does accountability work? Did I reach my goal?

Teach your students to set goals in their lives and write them down. Make sure they meet the requirements for SMART goals, then help them succeed. Two other things are required to achieve even the most air-tight SMART goals: Planning and Tracking.

Having a goal is great, but without a plan to achieve that goal, you're slipping back into the dream category. The only way to get somewhere is to know where you're going and to have a plan to get there. If I want to go to California, I have a thousand options. I could walk, bike, drive, take a bus, unicycle, take a train, carpool, tricycle, hitchhike, take a boat, fly, tandem bike, rollerblade, rollerskate, skateboard - the list goes on forever. If I'm going to fly, I need to first buy a plane ticket. Am I going to buy that ticket online, through a travel agent, through the airline directly or through a discount site? How will I get to the airport? Am I going to leave my car there, or am I going to have somebody drop me off? Who is going to give me a ride? How long will I be in California for? Will I need a week's worth of clothes or three days' worth? Where am I staying when I get there? How am I getting to where I'm staying? Every decision leads to another question and without a plan, nothing will get done.

It's funny because we look at that example and it's obvious that those are just requirements for travel. You might not make a list ahead of time, but you know those are the steps to take in order to travel. Yet everything in life is based around principles. If you want to go somewhere, you have to know how you're going to do it, and you should know what you're going to do once you get there. It's obvious with travel in that example, but do we do that with our greater life goals? If you want to own a big house, how are you going to get there? If you want to get married by a certain age, how are you going to get there? If you want to make a million dollars in the next 10 years, how are you going to get there? If you want to make a million dollars in the next one year, how are you going to get there?

Once you have a plan, you've got to track your progress. In the example of traveling to California, you can track progress by hitting the milestones in your plan, checklist-style. I decided to fly - check. I bought the ticket online - check. I booked a hotel - check. I found a friend to bring me to the airport - check. I packed my bags - check. I made it to the airport on time - check. I made it through security - check. Each checkmark on your list tracks progress.

What about your life goals? What's your plan for that big house? When are you going to own it? 10 years? Five? Maybe buying it in the next 6 months? What then?

If you don't track your progress toward your goals, you'll miss your target. Being one degree off from your target destination after traveling a thousand miles will put you almost 20 miles away from your goal. You want to keep track of where you are and constantly adjust so you stay on target. Storms could throw you off-course or slow you down. How can you adjust and make up for that lost time if you can't clearly see where you are and how you should adjust?

Remember, we can only teach what we know. I'm emphasizing the importance of setting goals, planning, and tracking for your own lives so you'll be able to teach those lessons to your students. If you want your students to be successful, they'll need to learn these techniques, and you want to be comfortable with them in order to share them with your students. So set yourself a goal, write it down and plan it out, then use your plan as a checklist on your way to reaching that goal. Your success will lead to your students' success.

Key Takeaways

- There's a clear distinction between dreams and goals.
- Use accountability with your students by finding out their goals and helping students achieve them.
- Practice SMART Goals yourself so you'll be more comfortable teaching your students.

FAILING FORWARD TOWARD SUCCESS

Open yourself to opportunities and opportunities will open themselves to you. Close yourself to possibilities and possibilities will close themselves to you.

One of the things that both frustrates me and breaks my heart the most is seeing somebody give up before they've even tried, dismissing an idea before hearing it, folding before seeing the next card. How can people give up before even giving themselves a chance? Why do people see yoga and say, "I'm not flexible enough for that"? Why do people who see something as beautiful and diverse as capoeira say, "I can't do that - I'm not strong enough," or "I'm too clumsy"? I hear it from adults all the time, a habit they developed as children, and it hurts me to see them carry that weight of helplessness their whole lives. This is one of the things we're helping to prevent in our students so they can lead successful lives.

One of my favorite quotes that I repeat to my students at least once a week is from Henry Ford: "Whether you think you can or you think you can't, you're right." If you think you can do something, you'll keep trying through failure after failure until you finally succeed. If you think you can't do something, you don't even put in the energy to try, and so you'll never be able to do it. If you want to do something, you'll find a way. If you don't, you won't. This comes back to the importance of neurolinguistics.

Not wanting to do something is totally fine as long as we acknowledge that it's our choice and not something that was forced on us. Take responsibility for being unwilling to be openly clumsy, inflexible, and weak for a time while you learn to not be clumsy, inflexible, and weak. It's our decision, not our inability, that stops us from learning new skills because we either aren't willing to put in the work or we're afraid to commit what's required for success.

At AMP Academy, we don't allow students to say, "I can't." They can say, "I'm not there yet," or "I'm still working my way up to that," but never that they can't do something. Every person can do anything that we have to teach - we just have to help them find the right path for their success, and they have to be willing to put in the effort to make it happen. You can go on YouTube right now and find videos of kids with one leg doing parkour or breakdancing, amputees with no arms swimming and winning gold medals, skateboarders with no legs taking massive jumps, people doing backflips in wheelchairs. These are the stories we want our students to hear. While people like that exist, nobody will ever convince me that they can't do something - only that we have to find the right path for them.

Nobody who is successful came to that success without a thousand failures behind them. It's okay to fail. Arguably, it's necessary to fail. Failure is a vital part of growth. Without failure, students won't have the emotional capacity to handle something that doesn't go their way. Without failure, they'll never build the strength to push through when something doesn't work out. Without failure, they'll never have the drive to succeed. Students have to know the discomfort of failure to appreciate the glory of success. Once one has felt the glory of success after pushing through the discomfort of failure, they'll continuously want to recreate it. The only way to cultivate a future success is to allow them to fail and teach them to fail graciously.

Failure is an integral part of the learning process. It builds strong character. A student can learn more from failure than from success, if the instructor asks the right questions. We want kids to think about why it didn't work. Once students learn to analyze and understand why something worked or didn't work, they learn innovation and can come up with new ideas to make it work next time. They'll be able to activate those analytical muscles in the future, becoming better problem-solvers and giving themselves new avenues for future success.

Because of this, in Ninja for example, I like giving a fairly easy challenge that 90% of the students will be able to complete, then have a more challenging obstacle that only about 50% will be able to complete, then have an even more challenging one where maybe 5% of the kids will be able to complete it. This gives them an obstacle to feel good about, one to challenge them, and one to remind them that there's always room to grow, to keep them striving for greatness.

As instructors, we want to walk them through their failures - not hold their hands, mind you - help them to understand what went wrong and guide them another way to triumph.

WALKING THROUGH FAILURES	
Instructor:	So why do you think you got stuck on the rings?
Student:	I didn't have enough swing to reach the next one.
Instructor:	Cool. How can you get enough swing next time?
Student:	Let go of the first one sooner so it doesn't pull me back.
Instructor:	Nicely done. Give it a shot and see how that works.

Remember, instructors don't just teach students how to *do* a specific thing. We teach them how to *think* about things, which will teach them how to think about other things, and that will translate into everything they do, because we as instructors teach principles. It's the principles of the things we teach that will affect a child's future success.

What are some of the life lessons - the principles - that you can teach in your everyday interactions with children and others? Share your favorite life principles with me by sending me an email at polvo@ampacademygym.com.

Key Takeaways

- Remind students it's better to try and fail than to never try at all.
- Use every failure as an opportunity for students to learn.
- Find the principles in the things you teach so you can teach more in the same lesson.

FAMOUS FAILURE FOR SUCCESS QUOTES

"Think twice before you speak, because your words and influence will plant the seed of either success or failure in the mind of another."
-Napoleon Hill, American Self-Help Author

"It's fine to celebrate success, but it's more important to heed the lessons of failure."
-Bill Gates, American Business Magnate, Software Developer

"Many of life's failures are people who did not realize how close they were to success when they gave up."
-Thomas A. Edison, American Inventor and Businessman

"I can accept failure, everyone fails at something. But I can't accept not trying."
-Michael Jordan, American Championship NBA Player

"My great concern is not whether you have failed, but whether you are content with your failure."
-Abraham Lincoln, 16th President of the United States

"Without failure, there is no achievement."
-John C. Maxwell, American Author, Speaker, and Pastor

"Failure is the key to success; each mistake teaches us something."
-Morihei Ueshiba, Founder of Aikido

"Failure… is the highway to success."
-Og Mandino, American Author

HANDLING EMOTIONAL OVERWHELM (MELTDOWNS)

A meltdown can occur when a student gets so overwhelmed with an experience that they don't know how to handle it. This can show itself in many ways, though one of the most common is breaking down in tears. Other times, a child might express their overwhelmedness through anger, self-harm, acting out, or shutting down. During these times, we want to help students to develop healthy coping mechanisms for these various states of emotional overwhelm.

Lots of books talk about how to calm a child with calming exercises, like deep breathing, counting, or other similar tactics, and these are perfect as immediate solutions to an immediate problem. Remember, however, that we want to have both immediate solutions and long-term solutions in our arsenal to wield as needed. I'd like to discuss the less-talked about techniques for treating the causes of emotional overwhelm rather than the symptoms.

The reason students have these expressions of being overwhelmed - or "meltdowns" - is because the child hasn't yet learned how to effectively manage their emotions. For instance, I've worked with groups from YMCA vacation camps and there's one girl who is such a perfectionist that she gets incredibly upset when she struggles with something, even if nobody else could do it either.

This little girl, we'll call her Emma, spent forty minutes of her open practice time working on a single obstacle during her latest visit - running up a six-foot high wall. Her dedication was genuinely impressive. The only issue was how she handled not completing the obstacle. As a seven-year-old, Emma expected herself to complete the obstacle that I put in specifically as the hardest level challenge. The angrier she got at not completing the obstacle, the less she used proper form and instead just threw her body at the obstacle unsafely. After more than a half-hour of trying, she finally reached a level of overwhelm where she became visibly upset, displaying through tears of anger.

One of the YMCA chaperons pulled Emma aside to do breathing exercises with her, and I applaud that chaperon for taking the time to help Emma calm herself. That's a caring instructor. As I expressed above, it's important to use both the quick fixes and the long-term fixes.

Once the YMCA chaperon had calmed her down and walked away, Emma immediately returned to the source of her frustration. After a single failure, her emotional state kicked into high gear again. It was clear to me that the calming technique wasn't helping because the problem wasn't that she was getting worked up - the problem was why.

This is where communication is imperative. As I said earlier, children have the capacity to understand what's happening to them, but they may not know how to express themselves without some prodding. Sometimes we have to get creative with helping kids communicate in a way that allows us to help them. I pulled Emma aside and asked her why she was upset, and she said she was upset that she couldn't complete the obstacle.

I asked her why she wanted to complete this specific obstacle so badly, and she said because she wanted to. Obviously, that answer couldn't help me help her, so I had to ask again. This time I decided to explain that I wanted to know *why*. We always have a reason for doing something, even when we don't know what that reason is. I explained we want to understand *why* we do something so we can decide what to do next.

She thought about it for a bit as I sat with her. The more she thought about why she wanted to succeed, the more she felt compelled to do it. She tried to return to the wall, but I had to stop her - she'd already hurt her knee by running at the wall rather than taking a step back to think about what she was doing and why. She clearly didn't want to think about why she wanted to complete this obstacle. Sometimes we don't want to admit things to ourselves.

After a bit more prodding, she explained that she wanted to complete this obstacle because she couldn't do it last time either and she wanted to be able to tell her mom she'd gotten it. She was seeking approval, validation, and to her, the more times she tried and failed, the less likely it became that she would succeed. She was building negative momentum, every attempt worse than the one before it because she stopped trying to do it correctly. To Emma, her tries with the correct technique hadn't worked, so she didn't need to try them anymore.

The difficulty was that the more upset she became, the worse she did the technique, and the farther she got from actually achieving what she'd set out to do. Now that I understood why she was so adamant about completing this obstacle despite injuring herself and recognizing that it was overwhelming her, how could I help?

For Emma's part, she just needed to be okay with failing. I explained to her that it took another girl three years of coming every week to make it atop the wall, and that girl was twelve. Emma was only seven, and short for her age. She could definitely still do it, but I reminded her that things take time. Strength takes time to build. Skills take time to cultivate. Patience is a skill in itself. I set her the challenge of being patient with herself for that obstacle, and gave her another obstacle to work on so she could tell her mom that she'd completed another instead.

The challenging part is that I know Emma needs this kind of help daily. If she were a student of mine, I could at least work with her weekly, and we'd see significant improvement in the way she manages her emotions within one to three months, as we have with all our students. Unfortunately, I only see her during school breaks, and that's not enough time to completely change her mindset. That conversation was a start with her, but this book is the greater move toward helping her.

The more people that know these techniques of seeking first to understand, then seeking to work through emotions with a child, the more likely it is that Emma will get the help she needs - maybe not from me, but from others who can help also, and we can all work as a team to lead Emma to a path of self-understanding, self-patience, and success.

Remember, children's thinking is just as sophisticated ours. They just have less information than we do, so we sometimes need to help them walk through the dark. Helping children to think about why they're feeling the way they're feeling will ultimately help them to come up with their own solutions. We may need to help them get there at first, but by walking with them through the forest of their emotions and getting them familiar with it, they'll eventually be able to find their way through that same forest on their own.

Key Takeaways

- Learn calming techniques for immediate behavior modification.
- Seek first to understand. Only then can you really help.
- Help a child to understand *why* they're upset for long-term behavior modification.

BEING CONSISTENT

I've expressed multiple times that consistency is key, and I mean consistency in everything - consistency between instructors, class structure, behavior, thinking, how we treat others, how we respond to stimuli, disciplinary actions for poor behavior, language, and attitude. Paradoxically, students need variety to keep their attention and help all learning styles, but they also need consistency to understand expectations. While varying workouts is good for strength training and varying the vocal tones and speech patterns keeps kids focused, having structure is crucial so students can feel grounded. A strong class structure creates a solid foundation, providing stability for new students and allowing older students to feel a sense of seniority and experience based on their knowledge of the system.

When discussing class organization and why consistency is important, we can look to Ivan Pavlov and Classical Conditioning.

Many of you may be familiar with the famous Pavlov's Dogs experiment, but for those who aren't, here is a quick overview. Physiologist Ivan Pavlov first introduced Classical Conditioning to the psychology world in 1897 and it has become a key component of future studies in behaviorism. The experiments leading to this discovery were intended to study saliva secretion and digestion while dogs ate. Pavlov anticipated the saliva response to occur when food was placed in front of them, but he noticed that the dogs began salivating as they heard the food being delivered. He soon learned that he could use anything to generate this same salivation once he'd trained the dogs to associate it with food.

I've noticed the same associative response recently with my own dog, a 9-pound Yorkshire Terrier aptly named Ares God of War. When I get up in the morning, Ares stays in bed as I brush my teeth, until the moment he hears my slippers drop to the floor. Then, he bolts out of my room and immediately starts jumping around my feet, excited for his morning walk. He's come to associate the sound of my slippers dropping with going for a walk.

In behaviorism terms, there is a neutral stimulus, unconditioned and conditioned stimuli, and unconditioned and conditioned responses. With Ares's walk, the Unconditioned Stimulus is going for a walk, and the Unconditioned Response is excitement. I drop my slippers (the Neutral Stimulus), ask if he wants to go for a walk, then we go for a walk. Consistent repetition has led Ares to associate going for a walk with the drop of my slippers, so the Conditioned Stimulus of slippers dropping to the floor leads to the Conditioned Response of excitement.

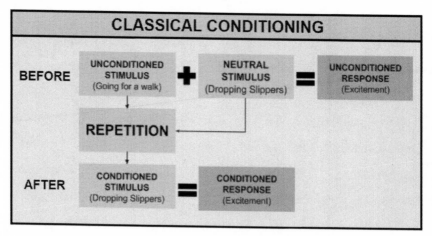

Consistency between instructors is critical in keeping an organized class. If I've given my students a certain set of expectations, those expectations will only carry to another instructor if the instructor does things that same way. If an instructor closely mimics my teaching style, then my students will treat that new instructor's class the same way they treat mine, due to consistency. If a new instructor changes too much, then students will test to find the new expectations and the class organization will fall apart. Consistency between instructors is the most challenging part of consistency.

If you send students to a task and have them wait for a countdown to start, while another instructor sends kids to their tasks and has them start right away, students won't know what to expect. One instructor might gently reprimand them for starting before the countdown, while another might gently reprimand them for standing around instead of working on their task. This is why standards are important. Every instructor should be on the same page, or the class structure will suffer, and therefore reduce the chances of success for our students. If you're an instructor working with other instructors, developing standards for the team will translate to better consistency between instructors, helping with student expectations.

Consistency in class structure is the easiest part of this topic. Keep your class structures the same. You can vary it slightly on occasion, but if you want an organized class, then you want students to know what to expect. In our classes at AMP Academy, we always start with a quick 3-minute strict warm-up, followed by 7 minutes of warm-up games, followed by 5 minutes of stretching, water break, then 35-40 minutes of obstacle or skill work with another water break halfway through, and we end with 5-10 minutes of discussion.

This format is so consistent that students immediately start warming up before even being asked, because they know what's expected. A few bits of well-placed positive reinforcement and now kids rush to be the first ones doing jumping jacks. Likewise, when we say to circle up after warm-ups, hands immediately reach for the ceiling because they know it's time to stretch. Parents joke about us having the kids well-trained, but that's exactly what it is - Classical Conditioning. Our consistency has led our students to be more prepared for the structure of the class. They're veterans at this point and set a great example for first-time students. They come in prepared to focus and work hard because consistency has conditioned them to do so.

Consistency of behavior and in our thinking refers to setting a good example for our students. Rules are for us instructors just as much as they're for students. Encourage students to have a positive mindset by having one yourself. If a rule is to not hang on equipment when the instructor is talking, then that also applies to instructors when others are talking. Be consistent in how we present ourselves on social media - oftentimes students befriend or follow us on social media. What we do in our personal lives on our personal social media pages is seen by our students. We must be consistent in our behavior there also to be good examples for our students.

Consistency in how we treat others is easily one of the most important. Every single child should be treated with respect and understanding. If we want to help children grow and become the most successful versions of themselves possible, treat them like the valuable people they are while simultaneously treating them like the person they can become. This goes along with the conversation earlier about equality - it's easy to get frustrated with students who don't work hard in class, and it's easier to hand out disciplinary actions to those students because of that. However, consistency in how we treat each student also means consistency in how we discipline for poor behavior. Who committed the crime is irrelevant - only the crime itself.

If the rule is no sitting in class and the disciplinary action for sitting in class is 10 push-ups after their initial warning, then the same must apply for a hardworking student versus an unfocused student. We can't adjust the rules just because somebody *usually* behaves. They may behave most of the time, but if they aren't behaving in that moment, they should receive the same disciplinary action for breaking the same rule. Every action has consequences and kids learning that lesson is vital for a successful future. Students who fail to learn this lesson as children may struggle to hold a job in adulthood or even face prison time for breaking laws.

Consistency in how we respond to stimuli refers to how we react to anything that happens in class. We want to always be a positive and calm presence around our students. If somebody gets hurt, remain calm, assess the situation, and handle it accordingly. Remember that students will react how you react. Stay calm. If somebody is struggling with an obstacle or they can't figure it out or they're afraid of it, respond positively and help them work their way through it. If a child isn't paying attention or blatantly does something they're not supposed to do, don't react with anger - instead, respond rationally for best results.

Consistency of language can be a little trickier. We're talking in terms of NLP and your language choices for helping children work toward success by holding yourself to the same standards of not saying things like, "I can't." Start listening to the way you naturally speak. Do you use any of the taboo words that disempower yourself or others? Do you use works that build others up and push them to achieve greatness? Do you use those words for yourself?

Finally, consistency in attitude might be one of the most challenging ones because obviously we've all experienced what it's like to have a bad day. Sometimes our fuses can be a little shorter, or we're so distracted by things in our personal life that we can come across as less positive and caring to our students. This is a super difficult thing to control, and it's by far one of the most important. Remember that whatever is going on in our personal lives has nothing to do with our students, and it's not fair to take things out on them, even by accident. We want to compartmentalize our emotions for the sake of the valuable and occasionally fragile egos of our students. Students often don't understand that our attitude from having a bad day has nothing to do with them, and they may take things more harshly than intended. Hard as it is, remaining "on" at all times will maintain our relationships with our students and help propel them toward their successful futures.

Key Takeaways

- Be consistent with your attitude.
- Be consistent with your rules.
- Be consistent with your treatment of others.

COMMUNICATING & INTERACTING

I'm a firm believer in good communication, both in my own interactions but also in teaching our students how to communicate well, which we'll get into more in the next chapter. Of course, I'm far from a perfect communicator - I misspeak and forget to tell people things all the time in my everyday life, but it's a major focus of mine when I'm teaching or working with somebody on a joint objective.

As instructors, we communicate with our students every single day, explain what we're going to work on, how to do it, and sometimes for behavior modification. Good communication is key when working with others, and this is no different when working with kids. In my own classes, I treat all my students as if they were adults, regardless of age. This means that although I'm an authority figure, I still value their thoughts, opinions, questions, and I still treat them with respect. I treat them as equals. I'm an authority figure, yes, but I'm also just a person, and so are they. They deserve my respect as much as I deserve theirs. Obviously, snapping at kids or commanding them to be quiet isn't respectful. As instructors, we have to trust that our students are intellectual beings and they deserve to be treated that way.

If we ask a student to do something, we want to explain why we're asking them to do it. It's a terrible thing to think, "They're just a kid. They don't need to know why I'm telling them to do something. They just need to do it." It's a very Authoritarian Parenting mindset, and we've already discussed why that's not conducive to helping children succeed. That way of thinking prevents students from learning and working toward the same goal as you because they don't understand what's trying to be accomplished.

If people do things without understanding the purpose, they'll never learn to find those things themselves so they can take the initiative to fix it on their own. Our goal is autonomy - independence. Our students should be able to see an empty bottle on the ground outside and put it in a recycling bin because they know that recycling is good for the environment and leaving litter laying around encourages people to litter more.

When people understand the why of something, they're far more likely to work with you. If children understand why we tell them to climb a box without using their knees, they're more likely to be conscious of whether they're using their knees. If they understand why math is important and you can give concrete examples of when you've needed it, they're more likely to listen, even better if you can relate it to them! Ask what they want to be when they grow up, and explain how understanding math will help them to achieve their goals. It could be as simple as, "You want to be an artist? You'll need to know how much time it takes to make a piece of art and how expensive all the materials are, then use those figures and math to decide how much you want to charge for your painting."

There's not much to say here beyond, "Treat children with respect, and they'll treat you with respect." If you show that you care about the things they have to say, no matter how inane it may seem, they'll remember that and meet you on the other side, reciprocating that respect.

One of my primary goals when working with students is to never say something a stereotypical parent might say if they were irritated. The whole, "I'll turn this car right around," and "Don't make me come back there," or "I'm not going to say it again," aren't useful when talking to children. They're all threats. Why are people threatening children? Remember, "You catch more flies with honey than you do with vinegar." Students respond better to positivity and rewards than with negativity and threats.

For communication, all we need to do as instructors is make our rules known and follow through on them. There's no need for us to threaten children. If the general rule is that being disrespectful will result in push-ups, then you simply give a reminder the first time they break that rule, and the second time they break it, just casually give them push-ups. Don't get angry at them. Don't get irritated with them. Just reestablish the rule.

"If you break a rule, you get push-ups. It's a rule to interrupt other students when they're talking. You broke the rule, so now you get push-ups. I'm not mad. I'm not upset. It's just what the rules are." The more calmly you speak, the more it reinforces that rules are rules and you're going to follow them. You're not angry about it. You're just following rules.

They get the push-ups out of the way and then they're focused at least for a time. Worst case, they break the rule again and get more push-ups. There's never a good reason to threaten a child. Threats are for those who don't have the knowledge or techniques you gained from this book. They're for people who think that violence and force are the only ways to demonstrate power or status. People who threaten others make weak leaders and bad instructors. It's a poor way to get results and a worse way to build good relationships with your students so you can have a positive impact on their futures.

Children are people, just like the adults you interact with every day. Try saying any of those things to another adult, especially one you work with, and see the way they start treating you. If you show respect to others, others will show respect to you. If you're disrespectful, however, they'll also return that energy. To give your students the best chance at a successful future, communicate with them the way that you want to be communicated with and they'll continue to learn and thrive under your leadership.

Key Takeaways

- Treat children the same way you would treat adults.
- Explain why things are done to help develop a sense of initiative and independence in your students.
- If children understand your goal at the start of the task, they'll work toward it with you.

ARTICULATING:

END OF CLASS DISCUSSION

The techniques described above will help you teach your students a positive mindset, focus, strong work ethic, self-control, respect, goal-setting, and confidence, allowing them to overcome failures, face fears, and cultivate independence, listening skills, critical thinking skills, analytical skills, problem-solving skills, and healthy coping skills, all traits that will help children on their road to success. The final technique I'd like to share with you with you here helps to develop articulation and good communication skills, which are the final piece of the puzzle we've created for success.

At the end of class, we sit in a circle and I give students the opportunity to share what they learned, a chance for them to reinforce the lessons they learned in class and to elaborate on what that means for them, whether on an individual obstacle or as a principle. This is also a time for instructors to teach the ultimate lesson of how students can become good instructors themselves.

Every student - every child - will grow up to be an adult - an instructor. Whether their job is working with children, managing a dozen coworkers, operating a fryer at a restaurant, or starting their own multi-million dollar business, they're going to be an instructor. They'll get to share their knowledge with others regardless of what job they take on in the future, so this part of class is a chance for children to learn effective communication. They may need to communicate over the phone, where they aren't visible to the person on the other line, making the ability to articulate and describe invaluable. With the indisputable value of articulation, why not start out as young as possible?

Most kids are used to being asked what their favorite thing was, so when you ask what they learned, they might answer the wrong question. If that happens, make sure to redirect the conversation to the actual question that you asked. Just asking why it was their favorite wouldn't address the question you asked, nor would it allow them to gain the valuable experience of sharing knowledge. Instead, say something more like, "Awesome, that's a really cool obstacle. What did you learn about that one?" Remember that the goal here is to get students to reflect on their experience working on that obstacle.

Useful Prompts & Probing Questions

- What different techniques did you try?
- Why did you try that technique? / What gave you that idea?
- Which technique(s) worked the best?
- Why do you think that technique worked best?
- Which technique(s) didn't work?
- Why do you think that technique didn't work?
- What advice would you give to somebody trying it for the first time?
- What advice helped you the most?

By encouraging students to reflect on their experiences, they'll use those experiences in similar situations in the future. For instance, monkey bars and rings are very similar. Wall runs, posting cats, and strides are very similar. Doing the first step for a wall run is the same as the first step for a wall flip. Each technique that you learn can be used in another technique - it's about concepts and principles. We want to help children see the relationships between things.

If you look down when you're on an obstacle, you're expecting to fall, you've given up and are looking for a way out instead of trying to complete the obstacle. If you keep looking at the obstacle, all your effort is on completing the obstacle. If you aren't looking where you need to grab when you run up the warped wall, you won't be able to reach the top because you can't see what you're trying to grab. Now how do those principles of obstacles relate to real life?

If you take your eyes off your goals, you'll never reach them because you don't know where you stand or how much farther you need to progress to make it. You need to build momentum on each of these smaller strides to build enough power to complete this massive jump. You need to build positive momentum in your life, filled with little successes, in order to have enough power to complete the massive leap toward your final goal. When students learn to analyze their experiences on smaller things, those principles will serve as lessons for their lives.

Once students have analyzed their failures or successes, it's time to articulate those things so that others can learn. Children aren't the *best* communicators, because they're still learning from all instructors who are also on a path of constant discovery and learning when it comes to communication, so a little prompting often helps them communicate more clearly.

Young kids often say things like, "You need to put your hands like this," using their body language to gesture. When teaching articulation, it's best to help students find the right words to describe something in case they can't be seen. Encourage students to describe what they learned without saying "like this," so they can practice describing things using only their words. This skill of articulation is crucial for developing good communication skills for their futures.

I like to offer the prompt, "Pretend I can't see you. Pretend you're talking to me through a door and you have to explain how to do an obstacle so the door will open." This gets their mind engaged by kickstarting their imagination. It gives them a task that isn't mundane like just describing something. They're describing something for a reason. It gives them purpose and it's something that very well could happen in real life. In fact, one time an AMP Academy instructor called me while I was on a business trip and asked me how to take down the slackline. I had to walk him through the process without being able to see what they were doing. In order to do that, I had to visualize where they were in relation to the slackline and explain what each piece looked like and how to operate it.

Sitting at the end of class also helps kids get comfortable speaking in front of others. It builds their confidence and helps them see that they're valuable and that they have valuable information and opinions. This also helps them build their relationship with you as an instructor more because it gives you another opportunity to praise them in front of their friends, building their confidence further. It allows them to practice being leaders, teaching others, and puts them well on their way to becoming instructors in their own right.

Public speaking is something every person will experience at some point, whether in elementary school, middle school, high school, college, professional careers - some people even choose to speak publicly, like me with my Parkour Mindset presentation that I deliver for elementary schools all the way up through colleges, focused around overcoming obstacles. Having children work on these skills at a young age is a great way to build their comfort and confidence. If a child can be comfortable speaking in front of people, there's nothing in this world that can hold them back from earning the success that they deserve.

Key Takeaways

- Foster critical thinking and give children a platform to express their ideas.
- Prompt kids to be more specific when you detect vagueness in a response. Having them describe in more detail is great for building successful habits like good communication.
- Our students are future instructors. Show them what a good instructor should be.

CLOSING THOUGHTS

As we go through life, no matter what our professions, we'll always be an instructor at some point. The purpose of this book is to give you useful knowledge and proven techniques that will allow you to become the best instructor possible, sharing your knowledge with children to help them on their paths toward success.

Use the Authoritative Parenting style as an instructor, high in warmth and high in control, setting expectations for students and giving them responsibilities to strengthen their ability for self-management and management of others. Have standards and remember to be playful - a child's mind is more open when their heart has already accepted you. Establish agreements with children to maintain focus and organization.

When disciplining a child for bad behavior, remember the 3 Rules of Disciplining Correctly: All disciplinary actions *must* match the crime, all disciplinary actions *must* be followed through, and all disciplinary actions *must* be followed by a chance to make amends. Disciplinary actions are good for short-term changes in behavior, but reinforcement is always better for long-term behavior modification.

Remember the lessons of social proof, learned fears, walking through fears, and exposure therapy. Children look up to you and want to be like you, so do your best to be the version of yourself that will help children develop into the best versions of themselves. Help them through their difficult moments by seeking first to understand and teaching them how to handle situations on their own, but never do it for them. Give them the tools to succeed on their own.

Only ever praise a child for something they actually accomplished. Don't praise a child for completing an obstacle if they didn't complete it. Praise them for doing an awesome job, for working hard, for almost getting it, for getting closer than their last turn, but never praise them for something they didn't do. Children, just like everybody, should be given what they've earned. Don't cheat a child's growth and development by giving them credit for something they didn't actually do.

All students are equal, regardless of socio-economic status, size, height, weight, ethnicity, orientation, preference, attitude, ability, etc. Treat all students equally. All students should receive the same level of respect and the same level of discipline if they break a rule.

Everybody learns differently. Get comfortable with the three primary types of learning (Visual, Auditory, and Kinesthetic) and remember there are variations and combinations of each. Train yourself to recognize each student's preferred style of learning by studying the differences in language use, and incorporate the various techniques for working with each style.

Help your students develop SMART goals by first developing SMART goals of your own. Remember the distinction between dreams and goals, and teach your students that every dream can be reached if they turn it into a goal. More importantly, believe it when you say it. Failure is an unavoidable step on the road to success. Teach students to embrace their failures and to learn from them. Only through analyzing our failures can we adjust and adapt and therefore ensure the future success of that goal.

Communicate with children in a way that will allow them to grow by being respectful of them, their thoughts, their opinions, and genuinely caring about them. Give them the opportunity to become more successful by giving them the opportunity to express themselves through sharing their experiences and teaching others.

Lastly, be consistent. The more consistent you are, the more your students can trust you and the greater impact you can have on their lives. You are a hero, and what you do is a gift.

I genuinely and truly believe that we have the power to change the world. Every interaction we have with a child is an opportunity to push society forward by helping children to become the best people possible.

Every child is capable of incredible things when they have the right support system to challenge them and push them toward success. Every question must be answered to the best of our abilities. Every positive thought embraced and fostered. Every dream changed from a dream to a goal.

If every single person in the world reads this book and follows the lessons in here, keeping the futures of all children in mind, imagine what this world will be. Share this knowledge with your friends, with your coworkers, with your families, and even with your children, the future instructors of our world. Pass this book along and give them the knowledge they need to grow and to help others grow. Together, we can change the world. Together, we can help every child live a bright and successful life.

CONTACT ME

Do you have any thoughts or questions based on the content in this book? Is there a child you're working with that you need more specific advice regarding? Are you struggling to keep your classes organized? Would you like to discuss other techniques that perhaps I didn't mention? Other techniques that have worked for you over the years? Shoot me an email! I'd love to hear from you!

If you'd like me to visit a local school in your area to present my impactful Parkour Mindset presentation to the youth of your community, helping them to see obstacles as challenges to be overcome rather than barriers to hold them back, contact me today at polvo@ampacademygym.com!

Made in the USA
Middletown, DE
14 April 2020